The Speech of Angels

Dedication:

In Memory of

Tommy Sova

and

in Gratitude to

Gary and Vicki Sova

for their generosity in sharing

their time and their memories.

The Speech of Angels

The information in this book is true to the best of our knowledge. It is offered without guarantee on the part of the author or publisher.

The author and publisher disclaim all liability in connection with the use of this book and the information herein.

ISBN-13: 9781493752393

ISBN-10: 1493752391

Copyright © 2013 by N.J. Irwin

All rights reserved. No part of this book may be reproduced or transmitted in any form or by any means electronic or mechanical, including photocopying, recording, or by any information storage and retrieval system, without permission in writing from the copyright owner, excepting brief quotations in articles or reviews.

The Speech of Angels

Thomas Carlisle : Music is *"The Speech of Angels"*
Author's Foreword

When my sister and I were children, we thought our parents were such worry-warts. They seemed to imagine danger looming over us and constantly repeated cautions about "strangers" and the rule against leaving our fenced-in yard. One summer day, however, a neighbor girl, my sister, (both age five), and I (age four) impulsively sought adventure by setting out to see if we could walk all the way to Eight Mile Road (about a mile). We didn't ask permission; we didn't discuss a return plan in case we actually couldn't walk that far; we just set out on our trek. As time passed, our pace gradually slowed until, whining about heat and thirst, we dawdled wearily from one shady elm to the next.

We assumed we had been really lucky when two nice Detroit police officers happened by and seemed to know, not only that we needed a ride home, but also exactly where we lived. Upon our arrival, we were amazed to find our mothers in a state of red-eyed, disheveled

The Speech of Angels

collapse, both dads home early from work, and the whole block in an uproar.

At first, everyone was really happy to see us, but, once we were in the house, Dad--using a tone sterner than we had ever heard-- lectured my sister and me and made us promise to never, ever again go anywhere without asking permission. My sister, being older, also had to take the rap for leading me astray.

After I had children, I understood what my parents must have suffered that afternoon. My own kids probably found me to be a worry-wart of imaginative proportions. If I heard a news story or learned in some way of a tragedy for a family, I sought an explanation—hoping to find a way to guard against, or to somehow avoid, a similar threat to my own family.

When a headline in our local newspaper reported such a story however, what had happened to that family seemed incomprehensible to me. I was acquainted with the people involved and knew them to be a well-intentioned, loving family. They had behaved in a way most of us would have: summoning the help they needed for their situation. If the Sova family's good intentions

The Speech of Angels

had resulted in a tragic death, could such a horror befall anyone's family? Occur in any cherished home? No matter how careful we are?

Years earlier, when we were new to town and were landscaping our yard, I often went to the nearby nursery, where I became acquainted with Gary and Vicki Sova. The first thing one noticed about Gary was his wide, friendly smile and his eagerness to be of help.

Since early summer is a busy time, and school was out, Vicki and their two young boys, Tony and Tommy were also there. Vicki, trim and pretty, with raven black hair and dark merry eyes, reminded me of my maternal cousins. We soon discovered our shared heritage of a Sicilian family background, a love of Italian cooking, and that we both had teaching degrees, though she had made it her career, while I had left teaching to work in our family business.

The boys, close in age to my two children, showed me around and helped carry my plants to the check-out. They were polite and helpful—not only to me, but to each other. I remember thinking that they were creating the

The Speech of Angels

foundation for a lifetime of brotherly camaraderie and closeness.

Over the next ten years, our acquaintance remained casual: friendly encounters, as happen in a small city, where there are visits to each other's place of business and chance meetings in stores or schools, etc.

The morning I read that disturbing newspaper story, I was bewildered by what had happened at their home. There were follow-up reports, official "explanations," but nothing offered me a reasonable justification for their son Tommy's death. After reading the court documents, having several hours of interviews with Gary and Vicki, and assembling details of that night's events, I am still at a loss for a logical interpretation of what had happened to Tommy. The tragedy seems as inexplicable now as it did the morning I opened the newspaper and read the shocking headline.

What all this information did make perfectly clear to me, however, was what his family and friends had always known: Tommy Sova was a remarkably talented, considerate, and gracious young man. His dedication to his music and the time and effort he devoted to it,

The Speech of Angels

beginning when he was only twelve, demonstrated the maturity of true talent. Considering all the attention given, over the years, to the night he died, it's time for the years Tommy spent as a son, brother, grandson, nephew, cousin, student, friend, and musician to be recognized and emphasized as his life's legacy and triumph.

Nancy Jurien

To the other Nancy
in the family.

Love,
Nancy

Prologue

Vicki Sova had been on bereavement leave from teaching for a year-and-a half when her family and friends, certain it would help her deal with her grief, encouraged her to return to the career she had loved for nearly thirty years. In the fall of 1995, she returned to the classroom, but she soon realized that memories of a place where she and her son had spent many days in the same building were too painful. A sudden image of Tommy, sparked by a familiar scene or scent or sound from the past, would flash into her mind and stagger her afresh with the horror of her son's death. These episodes sometimes left her so distraught, she was unable to finish her school day. She realized she was still too emotionally fragile to resume teaching and decided to take leave again before completing the first semester.

However, the next year, in the fall of 1996, Vicki tried again, and her family and friends hoped for the best. Vicki's niece was in one of her classes, and, while Vicki found the presence of a loved one comforting, she also felt a special responsibility, both as an aunt and a teacher, to help her niece with the demands of her honors level

The Speech of Angels

classes. Vicki discovered her body was able to get out of bed morning after morning; her brain could refresh her teaching routines and habits; her heart could still respond to the needs of her students. She felt confident that she was now strong enough to restore this portion of her life and the satisfaction it gave her.

Three years later, she faced a school year without her niece in class, but Vicki had been assigned to a new room in a newly-opened wing of the high school, an environment which held no memories. She was able to smile at a student's humor, sigh at another's antics, devise the best inspiration for another's difficulty. Maintaining her emotional equilibrium was a daily struggle, but each day brought the solace offered by her sense of accomplishment and pride in her work.

One lovely autumn afternoon, when the school fire alarm rang, Vickie sighed, some students laughed, others groaned, but everyone quietly began the drill which had become routine during the on-going construction of the new addition. Electronic over-reactions of small sensitive sensors being jostled by large clumsy equipment had repeatedly put everyone through emergency

The Speech of Angels

procedures and evacuation routes. What was different this day, with this alarm, was that it would destroy Vicki's teaching career forever.

Despite the suspicion that this was just another false alarm, Vicki and her students quickly performed the familiar sequence: close windows, exit room, shut door. She escorted her group to the left, straight down the hall to the north-facing exit. Since it also served as a landing for the staircase from the second floor, students bunched up at the exit door. Vicki didn't like the bottleneck in that vestibule, but, without too much delay, her students were outside the building and descending the few steps to the sidewalk.

As more students streamed down to street level, prior arrivals were nudged to the curb and then had to edge into the street to make room for the students still exiting the building. Vicki didn't think this was safe and looked for a better place for them to stand. She eyed the Church of Christ parking lot across the street. Since she knew the faithful had no need of it on Thursday afternoons, she led her group across to the empty lot,

The Speech of Angels

where they could all safely wait for the signal to return to the school building.

A couple of fire trucks negotiated a corner, rumbled up the short street, and pulled into the student/faculty parking area on the east side of the school building. Seeing geared-up fireman unloading equipment and entering the school, Vicki realized it could be a lengthy interruption—perhaps lasting until the end of the school day.

At least the students won't be cold if they have to remain outside, she thought. The late October weather was unusually kind: a Michigan Indian Summer wonder, full of blue sky and the Godspeed heat of a senescent sun. A blustery wind held the last of summer's warmth, as if gathering it up to carry south for the winter. In her short-sleeved shirt and long jumper, Vicki was comfortable without even a sweater.

When she saw ambulances arrive and pull up at the east exit, Vicki began to worry that the situation was more serious than a mere disturbance of electronic equipment. She shaded her eyes, and, squinting against the swirling dust, tried to see what was happening. A man was

The Speech of Angels

striding across the street toward her. He had white hair and a mustache and seemed familiar, but her memory couldn't find a place for him. Vicki wondered if he were an official with the fire department or with the school system emergency services.

The man carried his heft with authority and gestured with force, his open suit coat flapping in the wind as he waved his arm at Vicki and her group. He told her to get her students back across the street to school property. A sudden resentment toward him surprised her. She wanted to argue with him, question his authority, ask him to identify himself and his entitlement to give her orders regarding her students. But he had already moved on, gesturing and shouting at others, none of whom questioned his status. So Vicki acquiesced and led her students back to the school parking lot, where they were directed into the football stadium.

Vicki remained outside the stadium, pacing to and fro, watching the school entrance, where she could see students, apparently ill, lying on the ground. She glanced at the faces of students who passed by on their way into the stadium, hoping to see her niece. Surely, if she knew

The Speech of Angels

for certain that her niece was okay, it would assuage the anxiety welling within her. She approached the area near the ambulance and questioned another teacher until satisfied that her niece was not among the affected students. Then, she walked back to the stadium and waited near the entrance for school buses to arrive. She had to stay to help supervise her students' departure, but she found herself longing for home. Her anxiety, rather than fading, had grown into a sense of hovering malevolence.

Finally, at about three o'clock, with the last of her students dismissed, Vicki hurried straight to her car and yanked on the unyielding door handle. She sighed at her forgetfulness—she always locked the car at school. Her keys were in her purse, and her purse was in her classroom, and she just wanted to be at home! Then she remembered: When this had been Tommy's car, he had kept an extra set of keys hidden under the bumper. He had been a musician, his brilliance devoted to music; keys that helped create music were important; keys that opened doors or started cars were often tossed aside without thought.

The Speech of Angels

Vicki dropped to her knees on the gritty blacktop and groped the car's grimy underside. They were still there—the keys Tommy hadn't lived long enough to lose. As soon as she started the car and began to back out, she regretted her luck that morning when she had scored this prime parking spot so near the entrance. Now, a fire truck nearly blocked her in, but, with determined maneuvering, back and forth, back and forth, she squeezed past the glistening bumper, massive and immovable enough to crumple her puny fender if she misjudged the distance.

A few minutes later, Vicki was home, hurrying in the kitchen door and being greeted by Stevie Ray with the restraint and patient dignity reserved to cats of pure black with serene, pale green eyes. He had been inside all day, since Gary was up north finishing his summer project of painting the cottage.

"You want to go out, Mr. Ray?" she asked as she went through the kitchen to the sun porch and held the door open while the cat sauntered out. Vickie stood at the window for a moment, watching her pet dart around the yard among late blooms bobbing in the warm gusts.

The Speech of Angels

This was her favorite room, with its three walls of white-mullioned windows, bright tile floor, and the view of the lush quiet of their yard. But the comfort of her home and yard wasn't soothing her unease.

Vicki went to the telephone and called Gary. She told him about the students who had become ill and that the fear of a possible chemical spill or gas leak or similar type of construction-related disaster may have caused their sickness and resulted in the evacuation. She said she had seen a Channel 9 news van there, and, since Gary received that channel at the cottage, he should watch to see if there is a report. He assured her he would watch their six o'clock news.

After starting and abandoning several chores and fidgeting and pacing, Vicki decided to return to school. She needed to retrieve her purse, lock her room, and put and end to the unsettling episode. When she arrived, all the emergency equipment was gone. The school building was empty and quiet, her footsteps hushed by the carpeting installed throughout the new part. Vicki remembered how surprised she had been to see carpet in the hallways, wondering how it would stay clean, with

The Speech of Angels

hundreds of teen-agers walking through mud and snow and rain and then coming in while chewing gum, munching snacks, carrying drink containers. Actually, though, she mused, it didn't look too bad—yet.

Her classroom door was unlocked, and the room seemed just as she had left it. She went down each row, pushing in chairs, closing books and putting them in the desks, straightening keyboards, tucking away unruly mice and their leads. At her own desk, she gathered her purse and briefcase, and, after one last look around to see if anyone else had left a purse or anything in need of special attention, she locked the door and walked back to her car.

She glanced across at the church parking lot where the man in the suit had barked orders at her, and, on the way home, she concentrated on trying to fit the man's face with a name. Why had her classroom-honed memory for connecting names with faces failed her? And why did the failure seem to create such anxiety within her?

The evacuation of Mount Pleasant High School was a big story on Channel 9's six o'clock news. The reporter was shown doing interviews on the scene and he asked questions of the man in the suit, who was not

The Speech of Angels

identified on the screen. Vicki quickly called Gary and asked: "Who *was* that man? The man who was just on the news?"

The second she heard the rage in Gary's voice, the uncharacteristic language he was using—before she even heard him say the name—she realized who it was. The man who had spoken to her, who had shouted orders at her, at her own school, was the man who had killed their son—the man who had shot Tommy through the heart in their home—in her kitchen—the night of April 21st, 1994.

The Speech of Angels

Chapter One

Vicki returned to the sunroom and sank into a chair. She felt nauseated at the thought of that man having been close enough to speak to her. How could she return to a place where he may routinely be within her sight and hearing?

Mr. Ray meowed at the door, and Vickie automatically rose and opened the door for him. As soon as she slumped back into the chair, he jumped to her lap. Petting his sleek fur calmed her and also brought to mind the memory of their first family cat—the one of Tommy's childhood.

In 1979, a bedraggled, scrawny kitten had wandered up the driveway of the Sova home on Maple Street. Tommy, a nine-year-old with no resistance to the cries of small, helpless creatures, had scooped her into his arms—and into the family.

As her benefactor, Tommy was given the honor of naming her. He called her Mittens, and she grew into a lovely cat—creamy white with a black tail and butterscotch on her face. Several years later, one of Tommy's first girlfriends, who just adored that lovely cat,

The Speech of Angels

nicknamed her Miz Mitty Kitty, pronounced in her melodic Southern dialect. Even after the young lady moved back to Louisville, the new name, drawl and all, had remained with Tommy's cat.

Twenty years after her rescue, when Miz Mitty Kitty had survived Tommy by almost four years, she became too sick to live without suffering. Gary and Vicki took her to where gentle, competent hands helped her die peacefully. They brought the beloved pet back home, and Gary grabbed a shovel from the garage and headed to the breezeway, where Vicki stood with the shrouded Miz Mitty Kitty in her arms. He stopped at the breezeway door, which led into the back yard, and stared out at the icy January rain for several moments. Vicki assumed he was choosing a site in the flower garden for the burial .

Turning from the window and looking at the shrouded pet in Vicki's arms, he commented on the unusual weather, saying it made him worry about the rosebush they had planted at the cemetery this past year.

The bush had been thriving in the heavy Michigan loam at Tommy's gravesite, but if the mild winter suddenly turned frigid without the protection of an

The Speech of Angels

insulating snow cover, the bush may not survive. An experienced nurseryman, Gary insisted they should drive to the cemetery right then to dig that bush a little deeper into the ground and mound some protective cover around the roots.

Vickie stared at him for a moment, then, nodded in agreement.

Braving the gelid drizzle, they took care of that rosebush, which has grown more lush every year since its gentle unearthing and replanting that day at Tommy's grave.

Four generations of their family members rest in that cemetery in Mount Pleasant. Gary and Vicki expect to rest there; they were both born in town, attended its public schools, and had graduated from its local university. They married in its downtown landmark church, raised their two boys in the neighborhood near its hospital, and then, in the spring of his twenty-fourth year, buried their younger boy in its warming loam.

Years earlier, they had faced and accepted the idea that Tommy's talent would demand a wider venue than their home town. To fulfill his dreams, he would

The Speech of Angels

probably need to move away from this small city with its typical Midwestern history. Instead, he will never leave its soil, his life and death untimely spliced into the chronology of his birthplace.

The Speech of Angels

Chapter Two

This Mid-Michigan region's recorded history began with a journal kept by Jesuit Father Henri Nouvel during the winter of 1675-76. He traveled with the Chippewa Indians through the area of Central Michigan that would become Isabella County. They hunted and fished along the Chippewa River where the milder Saginaw Valley weather offered more protection in winter than the biting winds and bitter temperatures of the upper lakes.

Though Michigan became a state in 1837, this "middle of the mitten" area remained primitive until Congress adopted the Graduation Act of 1854, which attracted the attention of land buyers to Isabella County. With the price of land now set as low as twelve and a half cents per acre, even this area without roads or bridges or inns became attractive to settlers. It was also irresistible to investors with military land vouchers, which were redeemable for land made valuable by the potential lumber harvest in its virgin pine forests.

The Speech of Angels

By the end of 1854, the Missionary Society of the Methodist Episcopal Church felt compelled to urge, in a letter to George Manypenny, U.S. Commissioner of Indian Affairs, that the government should set aside lands in this area for the Chippewa Indians, before the opportunity to reserve land for the tribe was lost.

The Treaty of 1855, between the Chippewa Indian band of Swan Creek and Black River and the U.S. Government, did reserve from immediate sale four townships and the north half of two others—one of the two being Union Township, which meant much of what would become the north half of Mount Pleasant. Eligible Native Americans had five years to choose their acreage and some came from other areas of the state and even Canada to put in their claims. However, many sold their land immediately.

By 1864 new rules took effect, which limited what individual tribal members could do with the land they selected after receiving their patents. If an individual were deemed "not competent," he needed official approval to sell his land. The new Indian Agent, Richard Smith, was on his way to the treaty area to convince those members

The Speech of Angels

to refrain from selling their land. Mr. Smith, however, drowned when the ship taking him to his new post sank in a Lake Huron storm. Since no effort had successfully organized Indian holdings into a formal reservation, much of the land had been sold by 1872. In fact, more than a decade earlier a rise of ground near the Chippewa River had been approved for a courthouse, given the designation of county seat, and named Mount Pleasant. When first settled, it had been called New Albany and then Isabella City, and then finally in 1860 named after a town in Ohio that had impressed one of the founding fathers.

At 775 feet above sea level in a county varying from 706 to 900 feet, Mount Pleasant has no real "mount," and, in fact, in its more modern history, when the city and Union Township, which surrounds it completely, renewed one of their municipal feuds, some residents had even opined that it was not very "pleasant", griping that the two governments should just combine their jurisdictions—and their names—to create one entity dubbed Un-Pleasant.

The Speech of Angels

The newly established community began a campaign to make a name for itself to lure prospective residents, but one of its self-christened nicknames inspired ridicule from the Detroit newspapers. A pamphlet, published by area business groups and the local paper, *The Enterprise*, referred to Mount Pleasant as "The Hub" of Michigan. The Detroit papers made fun of the self-aggrandizing circular wondering why the state would need "another Hub" (when it already had Detroit) and casting doubt upon the qualifications of such a provincial area. If one judges solely upon a geographical criterion, however, Mount Pleasant, in the center of the lower peninsula, is certainly in a more hub-like position than Detroit.

A much-publicized trial of lumber barons, who had been accused of stealing timber from Indian lands, inspired another round of unflattering media attention.

But the barons also brought welcome growth for the local economy: saw mills, planing mills, stave mills, and shingle, sash and door, and basket factories. By the end of 1879, the railroad had arrived in town and, just as the Chippewa River had become the lumbering industry's avenue to profit by carrying logs downriver, the railroad

The Speech of Angels

provided a similar service for farmers. The crops and dairy products from the newly cleared lands could reach a widening market area, allowing greater profits for the farmers.

Over time, however, gratitude for the service which transports produce to distant markets can ripen into resentment at the cost of the service, and then the prospect of local processing becomes attractive. By 1893 Mount Pleasant had its own creamery to turn local cream into butter, by 1908 a condensery to supply the broader canned milk market and a sugar plant to cook the local sugar beets.

In the natural order of Midwest progress, the farmers prospered selling to local processors who hired people who needed places to live, and furnishings, and stuff to wear, and conveyances to travel in. What more could an ambitious community ask for? The riches of black gold, perhaps? Well...why not?

For the central Michigan area, it took three at-bats to achieve a strike. The 1903 oil "excitement" created the Mount Pleasant Oil Company and the Star Oil Company, both of which followed the Detroit oil speculators down

The Speech of Angels

to the Kentucky oil fields, where the boring results (pun intended) quickly calmed that area's excitement.

In 1912, the community relapsed into another bout of oil fever—but, this time, the exploration was to take place locally! *The Enterprise* began an "Oil and Gas Notes" column which reported the progress of the first well. This well, on the Riley farm south of town, produced a gusher of plain water, which cooled this second bout of oil fever.

Finally, in the late 1920's, a genuine oil industry roared to life in Mid-Michigan. The Saginaw Valley had begun yielding returns to oil investors, and eagerness for other sites to drill quickly returned attention to the Mount Pleasant area. It became the come-back kid of oil exploration. The Dundee formation, at about 3500 feet, was revealed as the stratum of lore all had been seeking, and its rewards and promise resulted in a local refinery. Now, the improbable "second hub" had become Michigan's oil capital.

During these years of the area's trials and errors of business and industry, the education of its residents had always been an important goal. Each summer, teachers

The Speech of Angels

had gathered at this county seat to listen to lectures on educational techniques at a County Teachers Institute. Visiting experts and educators were invited to present papers and panel discussions to the assembled educators and to the people of the community, who were invited as well. Many local people came to listen to the presentations, and some gave lectures themselves on the value of education in business and what should be expected of its public school curricula.

This interest on the part of the villagers fostered a determination to encourage advanced education, and a privately-owned Mount Pleasant Business College was established in 1890. Two years later, it became Central Michigan Normal School and Business Institute and, within three years, was accepted by the state as a state institution. After the disastrous fire of 1925, it was rebuilt as Central Michigan Normal School and dedicated to educating teachers for the state's schools. The college became Central State Teachers' college in 1927, then Central Michigan College of Education in 1941, and Central Michigan University in 1959, with a student body of about 4,000. Today C.M.U. accommodates more than

The Speech of Angels

25,000 students, retaining an emphasis on its College of Education, while adding a medical school.

The Department of the Interior had selected Mount Pleasant as its site for a school for the Indians of Michigan. The school opened in 1892 serving about fifteen students and expanded over the years to enroll 350 students in 1921. After years of controversy over the intent and usefulness of the national system of Indian Schools, the Federal Government closed the school and turned over the land and buildings to the State of Michigan, which eventually established the Mount Pleasant Regional Center for Developmental Disabilities on the grounds.

The Catholic Church also began its own tradition of education early in the city's history. A parish was organized in 1874, and by 1877 had its own church building and priest. Growth of the congregation and the building of a new church in 1882 allowed the old one to begin serving as a school. Sacred Heart Academy was established, and by 1906 served 300 students. Expansions and building projects over the years have made the church and school a landmark presence in the downtown.

The Speech of Angels

A natural supplement to the community's fostering of its educational institutions was its determination to establish a library. Mount Pleasant residents meeting in a lawyer's office organized the Library, Literary, and Musical Association in 1879. Citizen donations of books, fundraisers presented by the members, and annual fees paid by book borrowers created a busy 1000-book library. A fire in 1895 left the library and books in ashes and the Library Association with three cents in its treasury.

Failed fundraisers and disintegrating organization left the ambition of a community library on the doorstep of the city council, in the form of citizen petitions asking for support. In 1909, the council agreed that a library should be provided, and in pursuit of this goal, it appointed an official library board, which could solicit funds from everyone except, it seemed, the city council. Five years later, with 6000 books, the library needed larger quarters and more donations. By 1921, Mount Pleasant had a real public library, with its own full-time librarian.

The Speech of Angels

Providing exercise for the bodies, as well as the minds, of residents also became a concern early in the city's history. Talk about a public park began in the 1880's and in 1890 a proposal passed to sell bonds to establish a park. Across the river from downtown was a seven-acre woodlot, belonging to Douglas Nelson, which he had offered to the city for $900.00, with the conditions that it always remain a park and that its name be Nelson Park. Opposition to the terms and the location seemed strong—some thought it too close to the busy railroad tracks, some thought it too close to the cemetery, and some just didn't like the idea of its required name. But only 84 votes were cast against, and 340 in favor of selling the bonds, and soon the public had a park.

Another site with park potential was a low-lying wooded patch owned by Isaac A. Fancher and known as Fancher Flats. It was used as pasture for the villagers' cows, which were gathered each morning by a boy who herded them to the flats to graze. As the village's cow population waned, the flats became popular for picnics and the name evolved to Fancher's Grove, a name which

The Speech of Angels

seemed a more inviting destination for picnicking than "flats".

When the Normal School rented the land for forty dollars a year and created fields for competitive games for its own and the public schools' teams, the name became a stolidly descriptive Fancher Athletic Field.

In 1909, the city finally purchased the land. Their first project was the digging of a canal connecting the river loop around the flats, thus creating an island – and a lasting name: Island Park. Over the years, Island Park has had many improvements and has provided a pleasant place for relaxation or activity, except for the few occasions the Chippewa River needed it for flood plain.

The Speech of Angels

The Speech of Angels

Chapter Three

During these years of community creation, the usual tragedies of the natural world punished the inhabitants. Sometimes, as with the decimation of the Diphtheria epidemics of the late nineteenth century, where all the children in a family could die within a few weeks, population growth was affected. Even people who had survived sometimes couldn't face living any longer in a place of such tragedy. One man, after losing his wife and five children, loaded his furniture in a wagon, left it and the deed to his house at his mother-in-law's, and walked away forever.

The 1913 forty-eight-hour thunderstorm from Hell set hundreds of fires. It brought residents to their knees—hands over their ears, eyes squeezed closed against the blinding flashes, hair standing on end—to pray for relief. This frightening storm didn't scare people into leaving the area, but it did seem to have a positive effect on church attendance.

The influenza epidemic of 1918 closed all schools and gatherings and killed many people. Destructive fires

The Speech of Angels

and floods, horrific winter blizzards, the great ice storm of 1922 which devastated the entire county, may have all contributed to individual decisions to leave, but the trend toward population increase remained steady.

World War I seemed a remote concern for the somewhat isolated area in the middle of Michigan, but as tales of atrocities and bloody battlefields were told and written, drives to raise money for refugees were held, and recruiting began. A few local boys, too impatient to wait for U.S. involvement, joined the Canadian army.

By September, 1917, parades, bands, speeches, and crowds were sending recruits off to Camp Custer in Battle Creek to be trained for war. From European battlefields, letters were sent home by young men witnessing horrible death and destruction, with many suffering the former firsthand.

As reported in *The Enterprise,* September 18, 1918, the town's first young soldier to die had written (in part), as if from the afterlife, a poignant, simple letter to be sent to his family—just in case:

> Somewhere in France
> About to go over the top

The Speech of Angels

Dear Mother and Sisters:

I know you will be surprised to hear this news but I ask you not to cry as I have died for the sake of democracy's freedom for all.

I am glad to think that I have had a chance to sacrifice my life for something worth while.

The Redeemer has given me life and it is His right to call me back again at His will. I will see you all in the great hereafter.

Love and kisses. Good-bye.

Owen Barrett

The war ended two months later. Fifty-seven young men, packed and ready to be made into soldiers, were sent home; while Owen was one of thirty-five county men, already sent to the fight, who would never return home.

The town celebrated war's end in a typically small town way with ox-roasting and band-playing while a "yelling, tooting, cheering throng began a march and for a few hours they made the welkin ring". (*The Enterprise, 11/12/18*)

Mount Pleasant could return its attention to the business of growing into a busy, prosperous city. By 1921 city fathers and leaders had decided a more efficient manner of government was needed to meet the demands

The Speech of Angels

of growth, and an election was called to present the result of their efforts to the voters.

A new city charter had been approved by the state attorney general and signed by the governor, so, preparatory to the local election, the sheriff had "raided stills and confiscated whiskey" to set the scene for eligible and sober residents to adopt a charter "based upon business principles, a civic organization which will mean economy and efficiency". *(The Enterprise)*

The information provided to the city residents to help them cast their votes presented a favorable impression of this type of government. *The Mount Pleasant Times* was unabashed in its page one support for adoption of the new charter. On February 3, 1921 while notifying its readers of their obligation to vote on the charter on March third, the paper said the charter had been re-drafted "in accordance with desirable suggestions offered by".. (here were named professors and other " practical men.")

The front page of February 10th was even more emphatic: "This charter has been very carefully prepared after a great deal of labor by our Charter Commission

The Speech of Angels

and should receive a thorough examination by the electors.

"The experience of every city which has adopted the Commission- Manager plan of government has been that the cost of government has decreased and efficiency greatly increased.

"No city which has tried this plan has gone back to the old way."

The next week's issue (2-17-1921) printed the charter in its entirety on the back pages, and, on the front page, said: "The new city charter is before you in this issue of the TIMES. The more carefully you look it over the better you will like it. Disinterested authorities pronounce it the last word in a Charter for a city of this size.

"Already twenty-four cities of Michigan have adopted the commission-manager plan. All these cities are so firmly convinced of the superiority of this plan over the old plan that Mt. Pleasant will be taking a decided step in advance by adopting the new Charter. It will place the affairs of the city on a sensible, economical and efficient business basis."

The Speech of Angels

The week after that, the coverage extolling the virtues of the proposed charter had to share *The Times'* front page with the story of the shooting of a 16-year-old boy by police.

The two officers said they thought his car was the one that had been reported earlier being driven through the city street with its occupants firing shots. After shouting at the boy to stop, they fired at his car and a bullet struck him in the back.

The young man said he had just dropped off friends after attending a dance in Winn and was on his way home. He hadn't heard any shouts. No gun was found on him or in his car. At the hospital, the bullet was discovered lodged in his shoulder and "had not penetrated deeply."

Another bullet fired by the officers, however, had completely "penetrated the plate glass window of the C. E. Hagan store."

The other main front-page story of February 24th ran under the headline: "Commission Form of Government" and the sub-headlines:

The Speech of Angels

"Responsibility and Expert Management and Business Improves, Morals Revive, Taxes Drop, civic Pride Expands Under It."

Though no details were given about the methods this new government would be using to "revive" the morals or "expand" the pride of the residents, the article directed many questions toward "Mr. and Mrs. Voter," urging them to agree that the best way to run a city is to run it as they would their own business: "to hire...the best man obtainable...who with yourself would work hand in hand for the purpose of making your business pay dividends. That is just what the commission-manager form of government does for a city."

Though difficult to discern from this pre-election newspaper coverage, there must have been some controversy over the adoption of the charter. The issue of March 10th does refer to an expression of opposition, but doesn't seem to be enthusiastic about the role of healthy debate in a democratic society:

"The majority of 170 on the light vote cast was a decided expression on the part of the electorate of the city that a change of government was demanded. Not a word

The Speech of Angels

of disapproval to the commission-manager form of government was expressed through the press or in any public way until some time in the night's darkest hour of Saturday, a local mother-goose rhymer aspiring evidently to political notoriety (which he got alright) caused to be surreptitiously circulated a card on which was printed a poetical roorback on the subject of taxes. Evidently its author was a better judge of doggerel than of public sentiment. Mt. Pleasant has dealt with this kind of politics from the same source before in partisan elections and refuses to be hoodwinked by eleventh-hour tactics of this sort."

So Mount Pleasant settled into a manager/commission type government and was expected to progress smoothly from then on. After all, the justification for this type of government had been that the taxpayers get more for their money and that the responsibility lies in one person (the city manager) who must take the blame for problems and errors. This, of course, couldn't foresee layers of bureaucracy, employment contracts, and legal concerns, which may rise and grow and branch into a tangle of municipal briars.

The Speech of Angels

As befits a city with a new, efficient government, the community was growing in sophistication. In 1923, not only was the bounty on crows and woodchucks repealed, the Ku Klux Klan was publicly ridiculed when its speaker, having denounced the pope, was abruptly displaced on the platform by a local Catholic who ridiculed the Klan's ideas and called the speaker a skunk. The hall, rented by the Klan, suffered a mysterious loss of electric power, and the audience fumbled its way to the exits in the dark.

The city's image suffered a bit, however, when a representative of the Michigan Fire Prevention Association labeled the city's own fire building a firetrap. "I wouldn't keep a pet dog in that building," he said at a public meeting.

Because this was a city in the center of a county located in the center of the state, another problem became obvious: transportation.

Traffic census takers in 1924 counted 6,000 motor vehicles and 40 horse-drawn vehicles using county roads on a typical Sunday. Despite the traffic flow—and

The Speech of Angels

the new city government—spring mud still made the roads impassable every year.

Traversing the county to get from one area of the state to another was impossible, and local vehicles could make progress neither north, south, east, nor west. The county's fortuitous position in the middle of the state would never be exploited without good roads, and, finally, in 1928, many paving projects were begun.

Residents put better roads to quick use for the everyday school and work and church functions or for dashing to various phenomenon, such as a "gusher", for entertainment. Oil gushing 150 feet, as on the Lily farm, provided an exciting show.

The Joslin well, in production at the beginning of 1929, had carloads of people braving icy roads to view the 1000-barrel-a-day producer. The first oil well fire attracted an even larger crowd later that year. But in 1931, a gusher instantly changed the atmosphere from excitement to horror when an explosion ignited gas and oil and engulfed part of the crowd.

A reporter, Norman Lyon, wrote: "As we walked in front of the old county jail, a car sped down the street

The Speech of Angels

and wheeled into the Brondstetter Hospital drive. Two people got out, both yelling. We ran across the street, and Tom Caldwell, who I at first didn't recognize, said 'My God, the well blew up. They're all burned or dead.' Caldwell's face was black. His shirt was in shreds...."

Thirty persons were seriously or critically injured by the flash-fire, which lasted only seconds. None died immediately. But in the twenty-four hours that followed the blast, nine adults, including two pregnant mothers, succumbed.

Each death served to increase the magnitude of the tragedy and broaden the grief and shock that swept across the community.

The fire burned for three days, but, despite the danger associated with the industry, there was no snuffing the oil fever and no stopping a wide-ranging oil industry. Drilling contractors, field maintenance companies, and an oil refinery were natural results of the gushers.

While the "boomtown" atmosphere of the first rush of oil began to calm as production leveled off, the industry did provide enough growth so that the Great Depression had a minimal effect on the area. That and the

The Speech of Angels

presence of the university and a strong agricultural community attracted support businesses and retailing. From 1930 to 1940 the population grew from 5600 to 8500, an increase of 65%.

More residents mean more social problems, but local law enforcement seemed up to the task. Despite the burden of regularly enforcing the prohibition of pigs, cattle, and other farmyard animals on the city streets, the chief of police with four officers handled the civil and criminal load of 129 arrests during 1939. If townsfolk or visitors got too rowdy, the county sheriff and two deputies, headquartered in Mount Pleasant as the county seat, were also available.

Mount Pleasant was becoming a town of substance and taking its role as a city more seriously. It was already maintaining a safe water supply for the residential and business growth, pumping water from municipal wells and building water mains as fast as Michigan weather would allow. The Chippewa River, however, was still the major repository for the city's sewerage.

The Speech of Angels

Early in the 1940's, notice was given by the state that, at war's end, the city must have a plan ready to cease dumping untreated sewerage. Having mastered the municipal social graces of laying concrete, piping clean water, arresting and containing fires and miscreants, Mount Pleasant had only to stop inflicting its waste on its surroundings to clear this final hurdle of its adolescence.

Since the time of Father Nouvel, the area seemed determined to add population and prosperity. As the prospects of one crop or industry faded another came forward to rescue the area's promise. The sugar plant and the condensery closed, but grain crops and refrigeration kept dirt and dairy farmers on the land.

When Dow Chemical left town and decided to consolidate operations at its world headquarters forty miles to the east in Midland, the rebirth of the Mount Pleasant oil patch had soothed the trauma. The Normal School expanded into a major university and a major employer, small to medium sized manufacturing plants came to the area, and, as the twentieth century became the twenty-first, the Saginaw-Chippewa Tribe, which had become an entrepreneurial operator of one of the largest

The Speech of Angels

casino resorts east of the Mississippi River, began buying back the same lands the lumber barons had finished with 150 years earlier.

Mount Pleasant had seemed to make steady progress toward creating a city with much to offer its citizens in the realms of employment , housing, and safety.

Gary and Vickie had felt confident that, with parental guidance and vigilance, plus the usual warnings about strangers and boundaries, they had chosen a safe and nurturing community where their boys could grow up and prosper.

They have remained in their home on Fancher Street, the historic tree-lined boulevard where Stevie Ray (the cat, not the guitar player who had been one of Tommy's favorites) resides at the Sova home, enjoying the same comfort and kindness from Gary and Vickie as Miz Mitty Kitty had from Tommy for so many years.

The Speech of Angels
Chapter Four

In the four years prior to that rainy January of Miz Mitty Kitty's death, Vicki had visited the cemetery many times. One sunny afternoon, she had paused in her edging and raking and leaned against her grandfather's monument. Tommy's resting place was covered with the tender, satiny grass of a grave's first summer—its green not as mellow, the seams between young grass and old still ragged. His gravesite seemed youthful and awkward among the others long inured to their place in this silent garden of pampered flora and cold stone. Vicki began weeping.

The narrow blacktop lane curving past the family plot was lined with freshly planted nursery trees, their fat buds bursting into leaf. The warm weather and smooth empty roadway made a tempting shortcut, and four young boys on bicycles, their high, happy voices incongruent among the dead, pedaled toward Vicki. They slowed their pace and quieted their chatter as they approached her. When they were close enough to see she was crying, they stopped.

The Speech of Angels

One of the boys asked her what was the matter. Vicki explained briefly that her son had died recently and was buried here. The same boy, perhaps seeking a reassuring explanation for the death of a young person—like him, a mother's son—asked what happened. Vicki tried to explain the circumstances of Tommy's death. She said that sometimes young people become depressed and react very emotionally, and, even though he had meant no harm to others, he had been killed by a policeman.

Another of the boys, the smallest—he was only about ten—frowned and said earnestly, "He probably just needed help".

Vicki looked more closely at the boy. One side of his face was scarred, covered with glossy, puckered skin around an obviously damaged eye. She wondered if his precocious wisdom had developed during a painful recovery, when he may have doubted whether he would ever be happy again. He may have yelled at those around him, like Tommy had, that he wished he were dead. But maybe people had helped this boy and encouraged him—and now he was out riding his bicycle in the sunshine.

The Speech of Angels

No one with a gun had been there to hear his impulsive words and shoot him to death.

After the boys had ridden away, Vicki reflected that Tommy's gravesite was surrounded by family here—just as he had been in life—and that he surely would have received the "help" the young boy had spoken of. Tommy's parents, brother, grandparents, aunts, uncles, and cousins all lived nearby. His mother's and his father's families had been members of the community for over thirty years by the time he was born in 1971.

Both sides of the family were bound by their similar family histories, discernable here on the headstones. Their own birth dates beginning only a few years after the christening of Mount Pleasant itself.

Both sets of Vicki's grandparents were the first generation to live in this country. Her maternal grandparents, Rose Cavella and Joseph Falsetta, had each emigrated from Italy before they married and settled first in Pontiac, then in Grand Ledge. Joseph began in business selling fruits and vegetables, first from a truck, and then from the market he owned with his parents. Vicki's mother, Sarah, was born there, one of the seven children

The Speech of Angels

born to Rose and Joseph before he died at the age of thirty-nine on Christmas Eve, 1931. Rose was pregnant with their eighth child, and the country was in the first stages of The Great Depression.

Joseph had died of stomach cancer and some people shared their theories with Rose that she had caused his cancer by the way she cooked and the pots she used to prepare his meals. According to family legend, Joseph's mother, upon seeing her son in his coffin, had said to her daughter-in-law: "Wouldn't you rather it be one of those brats of yours, and not my Joseph?" Even though Vicki had, now, also endured a mother's grief, she cannot comprehend the cruelty of such a comment, if her great-grandmother had said such a thing to her grandmother.

Little wonder that Rose, even though she couldn't speak English and the Great Depression was growing meaner every day, took Sarah and the other children and left the only home they had known. She sold her share of the business to her in-laws and moved to Lansing, where she could live in an Italian community, walk to six a.m. mass and then to the market every day. Her decision—to bring her fatherless brood to Lansing—proved to be a

The Speech of Angels

good one. Her older children could find work and earn money for the family's expenses.

Rose could take care of the baby, the younger children, and the home on Saginaw Street. Sarah, being the second eldest, went to work and helped with the family finances. Her brother Bill bought a street-vending cart, did very well, and eventually became a successful businessman. Her sister Mary remained at home, never married, and had a forty-year career with the Secretary of State office. (People always said how it was nice that Rose, as she grew older, had Mary at home to take care of her, but anyone close to the family knew the truth was that Mary was fairly helpless with cooking and laundry and house care, and Rose took care of Mary's domestic needs.)

Over several years, Rose had saved enough money to have Joseph's body moved from its original resting place in Grand Ledge to a family plot she had purchased in a cemetery near her home in Lansing. She could visit his grave whenever she wanted, and, when the time came, they would rest in peace together.

In this environment, Sarah became an independent young working woman, enjoying many social activities with

The Speech of Angels

a wide circle of friends. She was in no rush to marry. Victor Fortino, the man who would be her husband and Vicki's father, was in no hurry for marriage, either.

Victor's father, Paul Fortino had been a teenager in 1906 when he left southern Italy to come to the United States. Though his brothers and sister went to South America, Paul went first to Michigan, then to Phoenix, Arizona to work on building the railroad. Meanwhile, his brother Mike had become disenchanted with the Southern Hemisphere and settled in Alma, Michigan. Eventually, Paul returned to Michigan, where he and Mike owned a market together and, with their new wives, lived over the store.

Paul's wife, Julia, had also come to this country in 1906. She had immigrated with her father, George Fabiano, from southern Italy to Michigan. He returned to Italy within two years to bring his wife and other children to his new country, and Victor Charles Fortino, Vicki's father, had been born to Paul and Julia when they lived over the market in 1915.

Victor was a rebellious sort, beginning when his father insisted on violin lessons for his eldest son. Victor,

The Speech of Angels

apparently unimpressed by his father's willingness to spend a shocking twenty-five cents for each lesson, managed to break at least one string on the violin each time he was supposed to practice. Paul Fortino finally gave up on his son's musical virtuosity, but still insisted that going to school was vital to a young man's success in this country. He walked his son to school every day to thwart his penchant for playing hooky. Victor, however, often sneaked out the back door of the building after his father left. Finally, the school system put a merciful end to Victor's educational misadventures by expelling him from the eighth grade. The family story says it was due to his inability to quit smoking—during school hours.

When he was older and away from daily family influence, he lived the life of a young bachelor on his own. Eventually, Victor could no longer finagle his way around an alarmed and angry father who had been hearing rumors of wild oats being sown. Determined to protect the family name, Paul Fortino decided the time had arrived for Victor to be married to an "appropriate" young woman.

Sarah Falsetta was suitable and available—in fact her parent's generation would have thought her past the

The Speech of Angels

usual age for marriage. After introductions and strong encouragement, Sarah, 23 years old and independent minded, and Victor, twenty-five and still stubborn, were scheduled to exchange vows, though apparently, the wedding had to be postponed once. (When Vicki was about twelve, she found her parents' original wedding invitations with the scheduled date a month earlier than the actual marriage. Her mother had explained vaguely that a death had caused the postponement.)

The wedding finally took place in October of 1940, instead of September, and Sarah and Victor moved into an apartment over the garage at the home of a businessman in the distributorship where Victor worked. Paul Fortino, who had moved sixty miles north of Lansing to the Mount Pleasant area, eventually convinced the young couple to move to Mount Pleasant, where Victor borrowed money to buy his own truck and go into business with his father. Victor drove down to Frankenmuth at night, two hours each way, to pick up a load of their breweries' famous old-world beers, bring it back to their little warehouse in Mt. Pleasant, and work more hours peddling the beer locally.

Victor and Sarah settled into an apartment over

The Speech of Angels

The Transport, a small downtown tavern. The beer delivery business was just beginning to prosper when Victor's father quarreled with a customer and decided they should find another location where he could count on people to be more trustworthy. This time it was Victor who insisted on remaining settled. He put his stubborn streak to use convincing his father to remain in Mount Pleasant, where, he argued, people were just as trustworthy as anywhere else.

Paul eventually became content with the situation. He could walk just down the street from his home to the warehouse everyday, sitting on a bench outside when the weather was nice. He grew a prolific garden, building hot frames to start his plants earlier than the Michigan weather usually allowed. Determined to grow a fig tree in the inhospitable climate, he built a little "tree house" with a heat lamp inside and eventually coaxed a fig from the tree. Carpentry, reading, and the thriving business he and Victor established kept him busy.

Over the years, he and Julia frequently hosted family gatherings in their home, creating many pleasant memories for Vicki and the other grandchildren.

The Speech of Angels

Vicki's mother, however, remained homesick for Lansing and her family and friends there. Victor and Sarah returned to the Saginaw Street house many weekends, and Vicki and her siblings have fond memories of the visits there with Grandma Rose and their uncles and aunts, going to big weddings and other interesting places. While visiting in Lansing, Victor wanted to go out and see his old friends, but strong-willed Sarah complained about his socializing. He would argue that he had a right to spend time with old friends, and they would each enthusiastically dive into one of their domestic debates.

Vicki remembers her Grandma Rose enjoying the gatherings and fussing over the food, making sure everything was fresh, still going to the market every day, and cooking, cooking, cooking. But even she found her daughter and son-in-law's bickering tiresome.

One day when Grandma Rose glanced out the window and saw Victor and Sarah returning to the house, she blurted "Oh, no, here those two come again!"

Their marriage, a blend of tradition, religion, and five children was strong and permanent, however, and, apparently, filled with a love enlivened by bickering.

The Speech of Angels

Chapter Five

Gary's family history closely parallels Vicki's, his parents also coming to Mount Pleasant in the early forties, where they decided to run a business and raise their children. Originally, however, Isabelle O'Neil and Levi Sova were from Cheboygan, Michigan. Levi was born in 1902, the first of five children, into the French Catholic community of Cheboygan. The same year, Isabelle O'Neil, Gary's mother, became the fifth of eight children in an Irish Catholic family there. The Irish Catholic community had its own schools and churches, and the French Catholic community attended its own places of worship and education.

Somehow, Isabelle and Levi managed to come to know each other well enough to become engaged, and they also found a way to have their wedding without creating a rift either in their families or the divergent ethnic communities.

Gary's maternal grandfather, James O'Neil, worked in a Cheboygan lumber mill and his paternal grandfather, owned a coal yard. While growing up, Gary visited

The Speech of Angels

Cheboygan often, and he enjoyed the time he spent at the coal yard watching his grandpa and great uncle work. Good times and bad, people living in northern Michigan needed heat in the winter, and since coal was the fuel of choice for those without a woodlot, the coal yard was busy. Grandpa Sova worked in a business suit and relied on his brother Joseph to load, deliver, and unload the sooty coal. Sitting at his desk in his good clothes, Grandpa Sova answered the phone and then hollered to Joe with instructions to take a load out to so-and-so and get back in a hurry to take one to someone else.

Great Uncle Joe shoveled all the coal by hand and delivered it with a horse and wagon. He never married and continued this strenuous work until he retired. Grandpa Sova died in his 70's, but Gary remembers his Great Uncle Joe still flexing his muscles, showing off his strength to the youngsters at family gatherings, and saying: "I'm 93 years old, and look—I've still got muscles!"

Gary loved his Grandma Sova and the giant cookies she baked, but he didn't enjoy his visits with Grandma O'Neil as much. He found her much sterner than his other grandma, and he had never had an opportunity to know his

The Speech of Angels

grandpa, James O'Neil. Like Vicki's mother, Sarah, Gary's mother, Isabelle, lost her father when she was a teenager. Isabelle was fourteen when she ran to answer the door at about the time her father would ordinarily arrive home from the lumber mill. The person at the door, however, had come with the news that Big Jim O'Neil had been killed in an automobile accident. That didn't seem to make sense—her father didn't even own a car. In fact, in northern Michigan in 1918, there were few cars to be seen. But, he had been walking home from work when an acquaintance offered him a ride. Not one to pass up an opportunity for a new adventure—like a ride in an automobile, he climbed in. Within a few moments, the car collided with one of the few other autos in the area, and Isabelle's father was thrown out the back window and killed instantly.

Gary's parents left Cheboygan soon after they married, most likely seeking economic opportunity. Levi was working for the A&P Stores in Pontiac in 1940, when they transferred him to manage their store in Mount Pleasant. Levi and Belle had two children, and by 1942 they decided the family's economic stability would be better served if they controlled their destiny by owning their own

The Speech of Angels

business. They purchased a tavern on the main north-south route through town and called it The Main. A man ahead of his time, Levi created a friendly, welcoming "sports theme" atmosphere with memorabilia and enthusiastic discussion, and the tavern was a success. A tavern is a demanding business, and Belle helped with the work, despite the demands of a new baby, Gary, who had joined older siblings Richard and Joanne after an eleven year interval.

Even though the family lived in town, as a boy Gary had his own pony. At the time, he wasn't sure why he had a pony, but, in retrospect as an adult, he speculates that it was likely because he was so crazy about movie cowboys like Roy Rogers and Lash Larue. Gary was mighty impressed with Lash's ability with his whip—snaking that whip around a bad guy's gun hand before any harm came to anyone. Gary was always running around playing cowboys and Indians, wearing either boots and guns or feathers and fringe, whichever was appropriate to his character. His father probably thought he was fulfilling his young son's fondest dream by giving him his very own pony to ride.

Gary, however, never became fond of his irascible, one-eyed Welsh Pony. He had optimistically named him

The Speech of Angels

Trigger, but this christening didn't instill any attributes of that worthy movie-star horse. This namesake not only wasn't interested in strict obedience or sophisticated tricks—he wouldn't even let Gary ride him. Gary looked after him and took him each day to the outskirts of town where he could be tethered to a stake to graze. Unfortunately, at times when no one could be there to watch over him, Trigger was tormented by a few of the local youth, who threw stones or even shot B-B's at him. This situation did not improve Trigger's temperament.

The Sova family moved several miles north to live in the country near the little town of Rosebush. They lived in a roomy house with Gary's sister Joanne, her husband Vern and their six children. Trigger could be ensconced in his own comfy stall in this quiet country setting, and graze in the open without any apprentice thugs nearby to torment him.

For Gary's older brother, Richard, and brother-in-law, Vern, a pony was not the appropriate choice for the manly pursuit of riding, so two horses, Pat and Chips, were purchased. Unfortunately, neither the change in living arrangements nor the example of proper equine behavior by

The Speech of Angels

the horses, had much of an effect on Trigger's temperament. Eventually, he condescended to join the riders and their mounts on excursions, but he preferred to trot along behind the others like a dog, rather than reform his attitude and allow Gary to ride him.

One day, Levi saw a sulky for sale and, thinking perhaps the pony had been trained to pull a cart, rather than bear a rider, brought it home for Trigger. This looked like fun to both Vern and Richard, but Vern won the honor of being the first sulky driver. Trigger acquiesced to the traces and even seemed inclined to pull the cart down the road --in the direction and at the speed--that Vern's handling of the reins indicated.

As soon as Vern turned him around, however, Trigger bolted for home, galloping wildly, ignoring the driver, and dragging and jolting both the sulky and Vern through the ditch and into the yard. Trigger must have had his one good eye closed because he thundered right through the swing set, wrecking the cart and throwing Vern into the air. Luckily, Vern proved tougher than the sulky, which was in pieces. When Belle came running from the house yelling "Now, don't you boys hurt Trigger!" the pony was assured

The Speech of Angels

of impunity for his bad behavior, and he enjoyed a quiet country retirement until Gary began high school and the family moved back to town.

At that time, another family was interested in Trigger. Levi told them he wasn't much of a pony for kids, but their little boy wanted him anyway. Somehow, either because he had mellowed with age and easy living, or the sudden bonding with this new family caused a reformation, the born-again Trigger became a well-behaved mount and lived long and happily with them.

Meanwhile, back in town, Levi had changed his mind about sending Gary to Sacred Heart High School. Just a week before the school year began, Levi decided that the public school would be better suited to his son's needs; so Gary began his freshman year at Mount Pleasant High, (where Vicki would begin the next year).

The Sova family business was prospering, and they bought a house in a nice neighborhood close to the high school and the tavern. The Main Bar under Gary's dad had the ambience of a family-type neighborhood tavern. They served typical "bar" snacks and had a crowd of regulars who made it *the* bar in town for beer drinkers. Levi would run

The Speech of Angels

ads for specials and make displays of the cases of beer, and people would come in for a beer or two and then take a case home. This was before the days of beer being sold in super markets, party stores, and drug stores. (In later years, a local beer distributor told Gary: It amazed me; your dad not only had the biggest bar trade in town, he had the largest take-out!)

Levi was a good promoter. He went to the other bars in town and bought drinks for patrons and started conversations and "arguments"—he loved to debate sports, politics, anything. People at the other bars would eventually end up at The Main to continue the debate with Levi and the other patrons.

Levi installed a television in the bar when most people didn't even have one in their homes. In 1951, in northern Michigan, many areas had virtually no discernable television reception. (In 1958, Gary's uncle, who lived in Cheboygan, had erected a huge aerial, but, nevertheless, saw little else but snow, winter and summer, on his television.)

The Gillette Cavalcade of Sports, especially its heavyweight prize fighting, was the sports phenomenon of the day. Levi put up a 27-inch screen, when the norm in

The Speech of Angels

homes was 12 inches, and put an ad in the paper promoting "The Fights" on this big screen at The Main for patrons. People lined up to get in, many of them driving for miles. Of course, in time, Levi also installed a color television when about the only thing broadcast in color was the Rose Bowl Parade.

The sports arguments at the main were good-natured and sometimes based solely on loyalty and devotion. But politics was a serious subject, though even intense disagreements didn't cross the line to angry confrontation. Since women were often present, either as patrons or working behind the bar, the rules of behavior were strictly enforced to keep the atmosphere mixed company appropriate.

One of the memorable election debates was in 1956, which was unique in that Levi supported and bet on the *loser*, Stevenson. Adlai lost the election and Levi lost big—allowing many of the die-hard Tigers and Lions fans to gain vengeance for the money they had lost on sports bets to Levi, who wasn't foolish enough to let his love of the Tigers cloud wagering decisions.

The Speech of Angels

Business was booming. Drewery and Strohs beers were the number one and two beers in the area in popularity, and The Main's distributor supplied both. Gary can remember whenever the Strohs and Drewery territory men came to town, they came to the bar and bought drinks for the house to promote their beers to the bar's customers.

One of Levi's promotions was to serve hot dogs and beer to the National Guard troops driving north on U.S. 27 for their summer training at Camp Grayling. Truckloads stopped at the Main, coming and going, every summer. Also, people traveling back and forth to their cottages stopped to take a driving break, have a cool drink, and see Levi.

Levi sponsored local softball and bowling teams, and he often took Gary so they could watch the games together. Gary loved it and especially remembers the softball game with Vic's market. The Main's team was well ahead, but the pitcher was tired, so a relief pitcher, a college student, was called in. Unfortunately, he didn't do well at all, and The Main ended up losing the game despite their substantial lead. The young pitcher had seemed very competitive and it was obvious he thought he had let the

The Speech of Angels

team down. Levi commented to Gary that the young man must be feeling depressed and headed down to the field to talk to him. Gary followed and heard his dad tell the young man not to worry about the loss; playing a good game was more important. Levi handed him twenty dollars (a substantial sum then, especially to a student). The young man tried to refuse the money, but Levi insisted he take it, telling him firmly that he had earned it. "You worked hard! You take that!" Gary heard his dad say in a way that left no room for argument.

By this time Levi had owned the bar for fifteen years, and the constant standing had caused problems with the veins in his legs. He decided to go in for surgery to repair the most painful of the varicose veins, expecting to return to work after a short recuperation. Belle was accustomed to helping out at the tavern, and Gary could walk there after school to wash glasses and help with cleaning. He enjoyed the task of cleaning and polishing all the furniture and painting the floor and, to this day, loves to work with, and finish, wood.

Gary's sister, Joanne, had also helped out as necessary and his brother-in-law Vern worked regularly at

The Speech of Angels

the bar, making a pretty good living. He was an easy-going man, a hard worker, and dependable. He didn't have Levi's jovial and boisterous personality, but the customers liked him and his quiet competence. The whole family could pitch in when Levi needed his surgery, so there were no worries about having reliable, trustworthy people running the business during his recovery.

Levi had his surgery in a hospital at Ann Arbor, a three to four-hour drive, one way. A couple of his friends went to pick him up when he was released. Of course, Levi had to stop at the tavern, just to check on how things were going. Things were going so well that he stayed until 2:30 a.m. talking and laughing and debating his customers. He hadn't gone straight home to sit and put his feet up, as prescribed. Then, instead of resting for the prescribed three weeks, he went right back to his usual schedule: Monday nights at The Elks, spreading good will for his business, and the other nights keeping the crowd happy at The Main.

Several weeks after his release from the hospital, Levi was struck with paralysis. Back in the hospital it was determined that a blood clot had caused a stroke—but he did seem to be recovering. Gary remembers visiting him

The Speech of Angels

and watching the Red Sox beat the Tigers on the hospital room television. Despite his disappointment with his team, Levi seemed much better, joking, as usual about his team's bankable bungling. He was kind of drowsy, though, so Gary left to let his dad rest. But Levi died later that night, his third day in the hospital. He was 53 years old, and Gary was fifteen.

Gary missed his father terribly, but he had to go to school, and he had to help his mother with the business and do everything his dad would have expected of him. After graduating from high school, he began classes as a freshman at Central Michigan University. After classes, he walked to the tavern to work each day.

But without Levi, The Main wasn't the same; people had flocked to the bar because of Levi and his promotions. Gary's mom and sister worked hard and his brother-in-law, Vern, worked especially hard, but Levi wasn't there, stirring debate and working the crowd, and the business declined.

One morning, the dependable Vern, on his way to the tavern, stopped at the local hardware store, bought a

The Speech of Angels

length of rope, and hanged himself in the bathroom at the Main.

The family was staggered. Vern hadn't seemed depressed or hopeless or unhappy to Gary, and to this day, he doesn't understand the suicide—neither the fact of it nor the manner—thinking it "the worst way I can think of to kill yourself." Many people may argue that there are worse ways to commit suicide, but, since the police had made him view the hanging body of his well-loved uncle, this manner of death has always seemed most horrible to Gary.

Joanne moved into town with the kids and rented out the farm. Gary had not been doing that well at college, finding that he wasn't even sure what he wanted to study, and at times, *if* he wanted to study anything. He decided to take a year off of school to work at the business, and he found he enjoyed the challenge of planning ways to build the business back up and increase the take.

The Main almost returned to its "old days". It still had its good reputation as a family tavern, continuing Levi's tradition of never putting up with troublemakers. Even when one of the bartenders, who was a competitive arm wrestler, had tough guys come in looking to challenge his

The Speech of Angels

authority, there was no tolerance for misbehavior. Or when underage college students tried to bamboozle a drink, or if liquor inspectors, dressed as deer hunters or fishermen or whatever would fit in with the current crowd of patrons, tried to catch the tavern serving inappropriately, The Main had kept a clean slate.

More and more people came in to join in the fierce rivalries at the pool tables. The intense games held people's attention and created interest within the community.

Other spontaneous entertainment drew crowds, like the night a local college student asked if he and two of his buddies could sing a few songs in the bar. Gary said sure, and Tom Tresh, long before he played baseball as a Yankee, packed the house at The Main, playing and singing as part of a Kingston Trio-type group.

Even though Gary was enjoying the hiatus from school and the work at the bar, he soon realized that he didn't want to make it his life's work. He had started dating Vicki and was thinking more seriously about his future and his education.

His mother was not happy that he wasn't going to college as they had planned, and she wanted to sell the bar.

The Speech of Angels

After Gary decided on a career—teaching—he told his mother not to hang on to the business for him. Newly inspired by his career goal and thoughts of a future with Vicki, he became a serious student and a success in his classes. Belle sold The Main the same year he and Vicki were married.

The Speech of Angels

Chapter Six

Vicki was born the second of Sarah and Victor Fortino's children. Her first home was the apartment over the tavern. Vicki has memories of walking with her mother to go shopping or visiting and of playing in the sandbox her father built at the foot of the narrow staircase, which led from the apartment to street level. The children could play there within sight of their mother. Also memorable was her father's fury when he discovered that a drunk leaving the bar had urinated in the children's sandbox.

That incident was probably the impetus for Victor and Sarah to move, in 1946, to a house on North Brown, a pleasant neighborhood of small homes with yards where kids had room to play and drunks didn't stumble into their play area.

For Vicki, this was the carefree time of playing in the streets and yards of a neighborhood filled with children. One neighborhood family had twelve kids, and that house was usually the first stop to recruit playmates for any sort of game or adventure. Often, Vicki and other

The Speech of Angels

children had to wait on the porch for the dishes to get washed before any of the kids could come out. As they waited, the smells from the kitchen, where the mother baked a dozen or so loaves of bread each day, wafted over them. For Vicki, this universally delectable aroma recalls her childhood summers of games and sunshine and energetic friendships.

For kindergarten and first grade, Vicki attended Kinney School, which is on Fancher Street (while Fancher School is, of course, on Kinney Street). From the little house on Brown, Vicki had to cross Mission (U.S Highway 27, at that time) to reach school. The children had the help of a crossing guard, but Sarah still worried because the street was so busy.

Once safely across, however, Vicki and the other kids enjoyed the adventures available on the west side of Mission. She particularly remembers stopping with schoolmates at a home where a man in a wheelchair had a candy stand. Vicki could buy her favorite coconut-flavored candy which looked like a piece of bacon with white and brown and pink stripes. The man with no legs must have supplemented his income selling penny candy

The Speech of Angels

to the local children, and the children loved the candy and the fun of choosing their favorites on their own. (Vicki wonders, now, what type of reaction, what types of suspicions of his motivation, such an enterprise may provoke among today's parents.)

Ordinarily, as a child in a Catholic family, Vicki would have attended Sacred Heart beginning in second grade, the lowest grade offered there at that time. But, Pullen, though a public school, not only had the advantage of being on the same side of the highway as home, but also had a guard for the one street Vicki would have to cross. For Sarah, the risk of the highway apparently outweighed the blessing of Catholic schooling, so Vicki attended Pullen.

For Vicki these were the years of zooming around town on her bicycle, often riding to Island Park for both summer and winter fun. Vicki thought it was really neat to have an island for a park, and most kids growing up in Mount Pleasant at that time remember it fondly—especially the swimming pool. Air conditioning was only in movie theaters, and for ten cents a kid could spend the day splashing in the pool with every other kid who lived within bike-riding distance and could raise a dime. Vicki

The Speech of Angels

remembers that pool being so crowded that "It was a wonder twelve kids didn't drown each day." She treasured the special times she was allowed to spend a whole quarter for the evening session, where there was space enough for actual swimming.

When she was older, Vicki enjoyed playing tennis at the park—except the day she accidentally whacked one of her classmates with her racket. She clipped him under the chin and knocked him off his feet—for which she still feels guilty.

Winter ice skating and sledding attracted kids from miles around and, though Vicki and Gary didn't really know each other at this time, (Gary was living and attending school in the country) they did have the enjoyment of Island Park in common. Gary had the baseball games with his dad and remembers the excellent sledding.

Even prior to the tennis racket assault, Vicki had a blot on her childhood conscience. The "Abandonment of Chuckie Episode" had occurred when Vicki was about eight years old, and it had instantly become family lore. One day when Vicki was watching her little brother, she heard fire

The Speech of Angels

engines. Momentarily forgetting her responsibility, she jumped on her bicycle and peddled down to Mission Street, where she could perhaps see which way the fire engine went. She stood on the corner by Gould's Drug Store. It had a soda counter, and lots of her relatives were in and out all the time. Aunt Lillian happened to come out, look down with surprise at Vicki standing there, and ask sternly: "I just saw your mother and she told me you were watching Chuckie. So who **is** baby-sitting?!"

Without answering, Vicki jumped on her bike and raced down Crosslanes, the most direct route home, as fast as she could peddle. Uncle Tony and Uncle Tommy and their families lived on this street, but she had no time to respond to any greetings from any or all of the eight cousins she may have passed on her mad dash for home. But—her mom's car was already in the driveway.

Vicki faced an angry mother who recited shrill examples of tragedies that could have happened to the precious son of the family. She made dire predictions of the punishments Vicki's father would devise as soon as he arrived home. (Sarah took care of minor infractions where simple, immediate discipline was adequate, but Victor was

The Speech of Angels

the official punisher of important transgressions, and taking care of Chuckie was *important*.)

Over the years, Victor had always called to check on the kids whenever they were in the care of a baby sitter. Vicki had seen his anger with any babysitter who did something irresponsible—like getting locked out of the house, which somehow used to happen frequently. Her dismay that he would be disappointed in her and her dread of facing his wrath is still fresh in her memory, though she can't recall what the actual punishment had been for her transgression.

Another crossroad in Vicki's young life was the school-choice crisis. Pullen only went through the seventh grade, and her parents decided she could handle crossing the highway on her own to attend Sacred Heart for the eighth grade. Vicki was woebegone at the thought of separation from all the friends she had been with since second grade. Every night for the two weeks that she attended Sacred Heart, Vicki cried at the dinner table. As the days had passed, however, she began thinking it wasn't really so bad. Most of her cousins went there, she knew many of the other kids, and she still spent time with her

The Speech of Angels

public school friends after school and during lunch, when both groups of students mingled in the schoolyards or went to the nearby soda fountain.

Since Vicki was adjusting to her new school, she decided to taper off the nightly tears, but, her father, had already reached the end of his endurance and suddenly announced: "I can't stand any more tears. You're going to public school!" Despite that she had been on the verge of capitulation, her campaign had succeeded—and one cannot refuse a victory after the shedding of so many tears. So, back to public school she went.

Sarah and Victor were careful with money, but they decided to be "extravagant" and build a roomy, brick ranch home for themselves and their children. When the basement was finished, they lived in it while the rest of the house was completed. Victor's father lamented that they were crazy to spend the enormous sum of $30,000 on a house, but Sarah especially felt that a nice home was important for a family, and she was not reticent in sharing her contradictory opinion with old Paul.

This was the lovely home where all the children grew to adulthood and Victor and Sarah lived until age and

The Speech of Angels

frailties forced them into nursing care. Vicki vividly remembers the day in 1957 when her father came home from the bank and sought out Sarah, who was down in the basement, sewing. He stood behind her and placed his hands on her shoulders. "Well, I made the last payment to the bank." There was no noisy celebration, no dancing around throwing mortgage confetti in the air, but there was such an obvious feeling of satisfaction and accomplishment in her parent's demeanor that Vicki's memory carries the detailed scene after more than fifty years.

Visiting her mother's family in Lansing and her father's family in Mount Pleasant was an important part of life all during Vicki's childhood. She remembers many family dinners and celebrations of birthdays and weddings and holidays on both sides of the family.

Grandma Rose's house in Lansing always smelled wonderful—always something with lots of garlic and oregano cooking. The younger uncles were still living there, and Grandma Rose was a warm-hearted woman who often had other kids from the family living there when they needed a home.

The Speech of Angels

Family celebrations with her father's family often centered at grandparents Paul and Julia's home. Julia had wanted to have a house on University Street in Mount Pleasant—considered by many a fashionable address. They had purchased two houses there, each of which burned to the ground. Paul insisted no more houses on *that* street, and they settled into the house on Mission Street near the family's warehouse.

Meanwhile, Vicki and her sisters giggled and wrangled in their rooms and cooperated in devising stratagems for softening parental attitudes about clothes and social activities and domestic obligations, the most important of which was still baby-sitting little Chuckie.

Of course, this boy-child's great value was not evident to Vicki and her sisters, who were getting to the age when their horizons were widening and a little brother was a pest, no matter how highly-anticipated his birth had been. Sure he was cute, but it seemed to them as if they *always* had to baby-sit just when interesting things beckoned in the outside world.

When the sisters were home with him in the evening, they devised a way to keep him up in his bed so he

The Speech of Angels

wouldn't pester them. When he came toddling down the stairs in his jammies, wanting to join them, they'd make the timer on the stove go off. It had an extremely loud buzzer, and he would scream in terror and scamper up the stairway seeking safety from the buzzing monster by burrowing in his bed. Vicki expresses guilt over such behavior now, of course, admitting that they "terrified the poor little guy."

After "winning" the battle to attend the public junior high, Vicki went to public high school, also. After graduating in 1961, she went to Central Michigan University in Mount Pleasant so she could live at home. The family finances did not allow for paying room and board to out-of-town schools, and, since Vicki wanted to be a teacher, C.M.U. with its well-regarded teaching program was the logical choice, anyway.

When Gary's family had moved into town, it had been his father's sudden decision to send him to the public high school instead of Sacred Heart, and, in Vicki's case, it had been Victor's sudden capitulation which resulted in her remaining in public school. These similar caprices of their respective fathers seemed to be the only thing the two teenagers had in common while attending high school together.

The Speech of Angels

They did not hang around with the same crowd, and they didn't really know each other well. Gary's impression was that Vicki was so pretty she would not be interested in him. If he had known that she thought he looked like Elvis, he may have been emboldened to get to know her better, sooner.

As it was, it took a conspiracy between Vicki's cousin and a friend of Gary's to create the impetus for the two of them to have that first date. Initially, Gary resisted, using the excuse that he thought she was "stuck-up", but admits now that he was just afraid of being turned down because "She was just so beautiful." By the time he had the courage to approach the lovely Miss Fortino, she did exactly as he had feared and turned him down.

Vicki had to refuse because she already had plans to leave for Florida with three friends on a trip to celebrate their high school graduation. Her rejection was polite, and too gentle to discourage him for long. Gary concluded she was more shy than snobby and decided to ask her again as soon as she returned.

Pantel's, a downtown dance hall in a converted Oddfellows' Hall, which had, in turn, been converted from

The Speech of Angels

a car dealership, was *the* place to be on Friday nights. The latest dance music played, the kids could smoke, some sneaked in beer, everyone hung out in the parking lot comparing cars and clothes—a real-life "American Graffiti" ambience. What more could young people of the late fifties-early sixties want? Everyone spent hours learning dance steps and speculating on who would show up with whom for this small town version of American Bandstand.

When Vicki had returned to begin her freshman year at Central, (Gary was beginning his second year), he went to her house to ask her to go to Pantel's with him that Friday night. This time Vicki had no prior plans, and she must have overcome her shyness, because, after that date, they were together as much as possible. In fact, the amount of time they spent together may have been to the detriment of Vicki's grade point average. She didn't work as hard at her studies and eventually actually failed a class: The Sociology of Religion. She placed part of the blame on the prof, who terrified her. She thought he looked like an evil Ichabod Crane, and he actually carried a whip and stood in the rear of the class and cracked it while exhorting his students to work harder.

The Speech of Angels

At the end of her junior year, her G.P.A. had fallen to 1.9, she was on academic probation, and Vicki experienced an epiphany about her education. She realized she would need 56 academic hours in the next year to earn her degree on time, but she knew she could do it—if she worked up to her potential. She completed nine hours over the summer, 19 hours each semester of the next school year, and another 9 hours the next summer to graduate on schedule—and with a more respectable point average.

She and Gary planned to marry that autumn (1963), even though Gary would not graduate until January, since he had lost time in school to work at the tavern after the deaths of his father and Vern. He had enjoyed the business, but it wasn't his career choice, and, since his mother also wanted Gary back in college where he belonged, Belle had sold the business.

The Speech of Angels

The Speech of Angels

Chapter Seven

Gary and Vicki decided they would marry the weekend before Thanksgiving. They could have a full week's honeymoon, while Gary would miss only two and a half days of classes. The Saturday before Thanksgiving was November 24th in 1963, so that would be their wedding day. Their joyful, celebratory plans would not fit the mood of impending national events, however.

Vicki remembers spending Friday afternoon preparing for the rehearsal dinner that night—probably doing something "I would have considered vitally important back then, like painting my toenails", when she heard the news that President Kennedy had been assassinated. Despite their shock and grief, the family had to rationally consider whether to postpone the wedding. Everything had been arranged and prepared for 500 guests. Food, church, hall, flowers, every detail was ready and paid for. People had already traveled to town. Flowers were cut; food was prepared; hall reservation paid. How could they cancel everything at the last minute? Nevertheless, Sarah thought they should. After all, she said, she had postponed her own

The Speech of Angels

wedding for a month because of a death—and this was a President's!

However, in addition to the difficulty and waste a postponement would cause, Vicki decided that their wedding had to proceed as scheduled because it was the only week-end that would combine with Thanksgiving vacation for a honeymoon. Holiday bookings would preclude rescheduling before January, and by then, Gary would be involved in final exams and graduation. So the wedding proceeded as scheduled, albeit with a much gloomier ambience than anticipated.

The Friday night rehearsal was funereal. At the church ceremony the next day *everyone* cried along with the traditionally teary-eyed mother of the bride. At the evening reception, most guests just sat talking about the assassination. Many frequently left for a while to catch up on national events, and they often returned to the celebration even more reticent.

Rather than the usual problem of over-exuberant wedding guests overstaying their welcome, most of these attendees left early, sniffling and dabbing at their eyes.

The Speech of Angels

Gary and Vicki had hoped to enjoy the good restaurants and shows and shopping in Detroit on their honeymoon, but everything was closed. As Vicki described it: "We could have shot a cannon into the streets from our hotel room and not hurt anyone at all".

On Sunday, sitting in their room with the TV on, they watched in horror as Ruby shot Oswald. On Monday, the official National Day of Mourning for the President, everything was draped in black as well as closed.

They were eager to shop at J.L. Hudson Company, the landmark downtown department store whose twelve retail floors and two basement levels would offer anything a newly-married couple would possibly need. They could have lunch on the thirteenth floor at one of its four lovely restaurants, then, later, have a dessert at the Mezzanine soda fountain. However, even Hudson's, the tallest department store in the world (25 floors, including its offices), which each year displayed the largest flag in the world on its monolithic facade to celebrate America's flag day, had gathered enough black bunting to drape over this facade for the official day of mourning—and had all of its brass and glass revolving doors bolted in place.

The Speech of Angels

All of the television stations aired the President's funeral, which expressed the deep sorrow of a heartsick nation, and the tragedy of a family with young children losing a husband and father was shared with the nation. People were truly grieving, and those of high school/college age seemed to be acutely affected by the assassination.

Not immune to the tragedy themselves, Gary and Vicki cut short their honeymoon and were back in Mount Pleasant by mid-week. They did not have anything planned for Thanksgiving dinner, and no one had expected the newlyweds to be in town. Even Vicki's parents were away. As would be expected in such a close family, however, Vicki and Gary were quickly and warmly accommodated at an aunt and uncle's table and managed to enjoy the holiday dinner with family.

The young Sovas moved into the apartment above the old warehouse building where Victor and Paul had first started their business. From the window, Vicki could look down into the yard where Grandpa Paul had grown his tomatoes and peppers and pampered his lone struggling fig tree.

The Speech of Angels
Chapter Eight

Vicki's ties to her hometown were as strong as her bond with the family members living there. Gary admits he would have considered living elsewhere "....except for Vicki, of course; she was here." So, other than a couple of years early in their marriage, Mount Pleasant is where they have lived.

In January, 1965, Vicki had to quit her job to complete her student teaching. Since Gary was still attending classes and only worked part-time, they could no longer afford their little apartment. When his mother, Isabelle, offered to share her house on Anna Street with them for the semester, they moved in with her.

Then, on Vicki's first day student teaching at the junior high, the roof, literally, caved in. The building was condemned, classes were moved to the high school, and everyone went on half-days. Teaching only half the day meant Vicki could have kept her job—but they were already settled in the house, the apartment was no longer available, and, having learned to be philosophical about best-laid plans, they remained in the house with Isabelle.

The Speech of Angels

When Vicki graduated in August of 1965, positions were scarce in the area schools. She found her first teaching job in Beaverton, a small town north and east of Mt. Pleasant. Gary began working at a Buick dealership in Saginaw, which would mean a substantial commute for him. They rented a place in Midland, about thirty miles east of Mt. Pleasant, which shortened the driving distance substantially for Gary, while only adding slightly to Vicki's. After completing her first year of teaching, Vicki realized she was pregnant and did not return to her job. Their son Tony was born in February, 1967, and they soon realized that a new baby in the family was expected to hold court in Mount Pleasant for family members almost every weekend.

With their hometown beckoning, Vicki was thrilled when she learned that a teaching position was open at Mount Pleasant High School. She applied immediately and was hired for the 1967-68 school year.

Meanwhile, Gary had graduated in January (having compensated for the year he had fallen behind when he worked at the family's tavern) and was offered a teaching position at St. Cecilia School in Clare, 14 miles north of Mt. Pleasant. With both of them teaching locally and the added

The Speech of Angels

inspiration of a child to raise, they went house shopping in Mt. Pleasant. The one they found, on East Maple, on a shady lot in a familiar neighborhood, was perfect for them, though Gary was already planning additions and improvements as they paid the deposit. Vicki was relieved that the house was only five minutes from both the high school and her mother-in-law's house. They couldn't believe their luck.

But then, the people who had been renting the house—and who had declined to take advantage of the owner's first refusal offer to them—suddenly reconsidered and appealed to the landlord to sell to them instead. Gary and Vicki couldn't forsake their visions of life in that house. They stood firm, and it became the home where both their boys would grow up.

Even though she would be very close by when her school year began, Vicki was still distraught at the thought of leaving seven-month-old Tony each day. "I couldn't have done it without Belle," Vicki says when she talks about Gary's mother, who came to the house each school day to watch Tony. Since Vicki was able to come home at lunchtime to feed Tony and spend time with him, the

The Speech of Angels

security of Belle's care for the baby gave her the peace of mind she needed to concentrate on her teaching for that school year and the next.

Vicki did not return to teaching in the fall of 1970; she was expecting her second child in late October. Gary, who didn't usually hunt, had planned to accompany his brother–in-law on the opening day of deer season, thinking that the new baby would be comfortably settled at home by November 15th.

The baby was almost three weeks late when Gary decided to cancel his plans because he didn't want to leave Vicki. She encouraged him to go, arguing that, with all the family she had in the neighborhood, she would have no trouble finding a ride to the hospital, two blocks from their own house. Gary would only be a few hours away, and remembering her lengthy two-day labor the first time, she convinced him he would be home that evening—long before the baby would arrive. (She was also remembering his refusal to go home to rest or eat during the whole 48 hours of that first labor.) Gary finally agreed with her logic and common sense and went off to the woods on opening day.

The Speech of Angels

An hour after he left, Vicki went into labor. In that pre-cell phone era, he couldn't be summoned from a remote hunting cabin in the forest. Vicki's labor was an efficient six hours, and, by the time Gary returned to the house, little Tony came running out of the door to greet him, yelling: "I've got a baby brother! I've got a baby brother!" The toddler's excited delight helped soothe Gary's dismay that he hadn't been with Vicki, and a dash down the street to the hospital assured him that both mother and baby Tommy were fine. (During the earliest grades, Tommy thought it was really cool that school would close just for his birthday—though most other people took advantage of the coincidental opening–day holiday to go hunting.)

Right from the start, Tony, a very active toddler, (fondly known as "a rip" in parental terms) took his duties as a big brother very seriously. He was eager to help with the baby and was able to calm his own rambunctious nature to fit the quieter, calmer new-baby venue. Even so, when it was time for Tony to begin kindergarten, Gary and Vicki were worried that he would not be able to settle into a school routine. When they went to his first teacher

The Speech of Angels

conference and the teacher began with: "Tony is just the *nicest* boy," Gary and Vicki glanced at each other warily, worried the teacher had mistaken them for another set of parents. Perhaps, Tony, having become the mature older brother, had calmed his boisterous personality to fit his role at school, as well as at home.

Tommy was a more contented baby than Tony had been, but, even as a toddler, Tommy decided that if something did not go as expected, there should be a reason. On a day when Sesame Street® did not appear on the television screen at the appointed time, he needed an explanation. He wasn't satisfied with his mother's speculations, so Vicki called CMU, whose local educational channel provided the program (ordinarily), and the likely incomprehensible technical excuse for their failure on this day, at least gave Tommy the explanation he craved, and he seemed satisfied.

Tommy learned his alphabet early and, probably because of Tony's example and guidance, began reading well before kindergarten. Tommy adored his big brother and couldn't wait to begin school. He'd be going to Pullen, just like Tony, and other kids were jealous of him because

The Speech of Angels

he had a great older brother who would look out for him. Being three and a half years older, Tony felt protective of his little brother and did all he could to ease his way in grammar school. Since Pullen went through the sixth grade, the boys were at school together several years before Tony graduated to junior high.

After big brother left, Tommy couldn't wait to graduate. And, then, when their cousin Chuckie also began junior high the year before Tommy, he felt as if his turn would *never* come. Finally, autumn arrived and they all got on the school bus together at Pullen for the ride to Junior High. To make things even more fun, they had BusDriver Bob, and they loved him and the bus ride.

At first, Tommy was a follower, with an older brother and cousin having cleared a path in the new school. But soon, Tommy made lots of new friends on his own. He also liked his teachers, especially Mrs. Wheeler (dubbed Granny Wheels), and overall he enjoyed junior high.

He loved reading, evolving his tastes as he matured: from Dennis the Menace, to Judy Blume, and, as a teenager, the *Mad Magazine* crew. Both boys were always well behaved in school, and Vicki doesn't remember either one

The Speech of Angels

having detentions. In this atmosphere, Tommy's love of learning naturally led to his earning all A's in his classes, and he became ripe for an interest to challenge his creativity.

Vicki began wondering if he would be ready to revive his interest in music. When he was only five, Tommy had asked if he could have a harmonica. His request surprised her, but she got him the harmonica. He lost interest in it fairly quickly, which wasn't surprising considering his age, but he must have felt a response within himself to music. He asked for a piano when he was about seven. An investment this substantial would need a preliminary audition. Vicki offered Tommy piano lessons, but he would have to practice on the piano at Pullen School after classes until she was certain of his commitment. Though it lasted longer than his previous harmonic adventure, Tommy's devotion faded and did not survive summer's outdoor attractions. Vicki, however, had been convinced that he had a genuine interest in music.

Schafer Music was down the block and across Mission Road from their home, and one day, close to Christmas, as Vicki and Tony left the house for some

The Speech of Angels

shopping, she had a sudden thought. She mused to Tony: "I'm short one gift for Tommy; do you think he'd like a guitar?" Tony replied "Hey! He might!" with quick enthusiasm.

Though neither she nor Tony knew anything about such things, they went straight to the music store, and Vicki spent about $120.00 on what she considered a kind of wild-looking used guitar. She also bought an amplifier, thinking that it would be vital to a young man on the cusp of teenhood. After Tommy held that guitar, at his twelfth Christmas celebration, he was never again without a guitar close by. He had been introduced to--and fallen in love with--the instrument his latent talent had been seeking.

He seemed to have little interest in the amplifier, and, after Vicki heard his first strumming, she thought it might be just as well. "There's no hope here," she remembers thinking, but, allowing for a talent which would respond to the proper coaxing, she went back to Schafer music and arranged lessons for Tommy. He attended faithfully and practiced for hours alone in his second-floor room. Since he still eschewed amplification, the rest of the family barely heard his playing from downstairs.

The Speech of Angels

Six months later, the weather was warm, the windows were open, and Vicki and Tony were sitting in the living room. They heard the unmistakable opening riff to Ozzy Osbourne's *Crazy Train*. They looked at each other; it wasn't the actual recording, but it was really good! Could that actually be Tommy playing? He must have finally put on the amps so they could hear him, and suddenly he could really PLAY! (Of course, it didn't seem "sudden" to Tommy, after his months of devoted, but quiet, practice for hours on end.)

From then on, his family and friends associated that opening riff with Tommy—his "trademark" song. (In recent years, Vicki was startled to again hear *Crazy Train*—as part of a car commercial. Then she realized it made perfect sense: Tommy's generation would be the right age for such a product and that song would grab their attention. If Tommy had been alive, he certainly would have taken notice, but, whether to react favorably towards the car or resent the commercial use of the song, it would be difficult to say.

Vicki and Gary began to realize that Tommy had genuine talent and sought lessons which would offer more

The Speech of Angels

sophistication. A CMU music professor, who played the lute and guitar, was reluctant at first, since the boy was only twelve (probably thinking he wanted to be a heavy-metal head-banger), but Tommy insisted his ambition was to study Classic Guitar. The teacher was impressed, and an arrangement was made.

Vicki and Gary purchased a classical guitar and agreed to pay $15.00 per one-half hour session, which, considering most lessons were half that for a full hour, was a hefty fee in 1982, and, in family legend, lacking Tommy's talent and dedication, his grandpa's aborted violin lessons had proven exorbitant at 25 cents!

The Speech of Angels

The Speech of Angels

Chapter Nine

At first, at the stroke ending the half hour lesson, Tommy would be ushered out the door. Since he was ready to devote himself to this music and worked diligently, his teacher soon became more intent upon the lessons, often keeping Tommy longer than the allotted time. Classical Guitar is a difficult and serious ambition—an intense study for a twelve-year-old boy to undertake. He must learn to play classical music using the proper method on a proper Classic Guitar, an instrument built for this style of music and fingering.

The neck is wider to allow more distance between the strings for the fingers to "pluck" them, rather than strum or use a pick. The strings are made of nylon to allow the guitarist to use both the fingernails and the finger tips on them to create the exact expression of the music. The construction of the guitar allows the top of the neck to vibrate, but the rest of the neck and the sides and back suppress the vibration allowing the center to resonate and project the full potential of the sound.

The Speech of Angels

Without amplification the Classical Guitar can achieve the volume and clarity of sound needed to perform the music in auditoriums and other stage venues, while doing justice to the composer, the performer, and the audience.

The teacher commented that Tommy had good hands for Classical Guitar, which is very structured and demands a certain hand frame and form, in addition to talent. When this teacher left the university, he encouraged Tommy to continue his study, but he cautioned: Don't let anyone teach you any other method except the Segovian Method.

Andres Segovia (1893-1987) was considered the father of the modern classical guitar movement. He believed this instrument should truly be studied seriously at universities. Despite the objections of his family (They wanted him to play a "real" instrument.), he devoted his life to classical guitar and brought his music to stages throughout the world. His mastery of the guitar and the beauty of the music gave it a status usually reserved for the violin and the piano. He had developed a method of study for the classical guitar which included lengthy and

The Speech of Angels

diligent practice of scales and had designed a system of exercises and practice to help the student progress by training first the hands and then the mind to accomplish mastery of the instrument.

His method recommended at least two hours a day in the study of scales, which would strengthen the fingers and add the elasticity to the joints needed to gain the speed and accuracy needed to play Classical Guitar. He gave careful instructions on the proper shaping and length of the fingernails of each hand to achieve the proper pressure on, or plucking of, the strings.

It was important to Tommy to continue this training, so Vicki had to find another program which offered the right method--and a teacher willing to accept a young student. A natural choice would be the famed Interlochen Center for the Arts, in Northern Michigan, but its musical curriculum was not offering instruction in the Segovian method.

Vicki then contacted Michigan State University and drove Tommy to Lansing for an audition and interview. After Tommy played, the instructor commented: Well, the boy certainly has wonderful hands;

The Speech of Angels

let's find out what's in his head. So, Tommy was accepted as a student, and Vicki drove him to Lansing every week, an hour each way.

It was on this drive each week that Vicki became accustomed to the change in Tommy's pre- and post-performance personality. On the ride to the lesson, he was tense and nervous, but, on the way home, his lesson and performance completed to his satisfaction, he was jubilant and talkative. The morose, jittery boy traveled south, but the happy, goofy kid came back home with her.

During this time, Tommy learned that Andres Sogovia was actually going to give a performance in Ann Arbor. Tommy was sixteen and had just received his driver's license, but he knew his parents would not allow him to make the five-hour round trip on his own.

He begged his mother to take him to see the great man perform. She fretted because they would be out so late on a school night, but she recognized this was an opportunity of a lifetime for her son: He would see a performance of the music which meant so much to him—by the man who had developed its modern form.

Vicki managed to obtain two tickets, though on

The Speech of Angels

such short notice, the seats were the least desirable.

When they arrived at the theater, Tommy encouraged his mother to ask at the box office if any better seats were now available. "Maybe someone couldn't come, and we could get their tickets!"

As it happened, that "someone" who couldn't make the performance had fourth row center seats—their new seats would be right in front of Segovia! Then, Tommy suggested that they should go around to the back to see Segovia arrive. Vicki was surprised by her son's initiative, which was rewarded when a car drove up near the back door, and they saw Segovia, himself, enter the theater.

When the lady behind the wheel pulled away to park, Tommy followed the car, and, as soon as she stepped from it, he ran up to her. (Vicki was flabbergasted at his boldness; he was usually so shy he seldom spoke spontaneously, much less to a stranger.) He offered his program to the lady and blurted, "I came all the way from Mount Pleasant to hear Mr. Segovia! Could you get him to sign my program, please?"

The lady explained that Mr. Segovia was usually

The Speech of Angels

pretty tense and nervous before a concert, (which Tommy could relate to), but she took the program and said she would ask him afterward. "I'll be back!" Tommy assured her.

Their seats were great. Mr. Segovia, who was in his nineties, had to be helped on the stage, but once he began his performance, he seemed full of youthful animation. Tommy, his face as animated as his idol's, sat on the edge of his seat watching every movement of Segovia's hands. After his performance, as they were applauding, Vicki leaned towards Tommy and asked, "Well, what did you think?"

Tommy, still clapping enthusiastically, replied, "He's great! But it might be because he's so old, I think he might have made a couple of mistakes." As the applause finished, Tommy suggested that they go out the side door. "We might see him when he comes out!"

They were standing at the back, waiting, when a man opened the back door and asked: "Where's the young man from Mount Pleasant?"

"That's me!" Tommy stepped right up, hoping to receive his signed program.

The Speech of Angels

Instead, the man invited them in! "Mr. Segovia would like to meet you," he explained, holding the door wide. Mr. Segovia stood when they entered and shook hands with Tommy. Since Segovia didn't speak much English, the other man explained to Tommy that Mr. Segovia was very interested in encouraging young people. "We don't see many people your age at his concerts anymore, and he wanted to meet you." Segovia signed Tommy's program and spoke a few words of encouragement to him.

Tommy was thrilled well in excess of his hopes for an impersonal autograph. It meant the world to a young man who had worked so hard to learn the methods and techniques of such a master to actually meet him, and, then, in addition, to hear such kind words from him was overwhelming.

The next day, in the Detroit papers, Segovia announced that he wished to return to Ann Arbor to play for the same audience again. He didn't think he had played flawlessly, and he wanted to make it up to them. Tommy commented to his mother, "Wow, I really did see a couple of mistakes." Tommy was eager for another

The Speech of Angels

chance to see the great master perform, but Segovia died before he could return for another concert.

When Tommy was still a junior in high school, he learned that Alma College, well-known for its music curriculum and performances, was planning to offer a scholarship in classical guitar. Since his teacher had decided to leave MSU, Tommy was without an appropriate instructor to help him prepare for such a challenging audition. Studying for such an ambition without any formal training was daunting, but Tommy studied and practiced--on his own--for the next two years.

During these hours alone, it must have been of some comfort to know that Segovia, himself, had studied alone and had, indeed, gained an incredible mastery of the instrument. Tommy had an instruction book, written by the master himself, for young students of the Classical Guitar who had to study without a qualified instructor.

This text covered the rudiments of musical instruction and practice, down to the important details of manicuring the fingernails. Though Tommy had progressed well beyond this level of instruction, the book's photos of Segovia teaching children and the many

The Speech of Angels

musical exercises depicted to perfect technical development were not only still useful, but must have been inspiring. Imagine Tommy reading in Segovia's own words how he, at a similar age, had been both pupil and master respectively, but so talented and dedicated that he had presented his first concert at the age of sixteen.

Tommy practiced every possible moment until his scheduled performance date. His intense concentration during hours of practice was draining, and he became edgy as the time approached for him to play for the scholarship jury. Vicki remembers his attention to every detail, including his insistence on the proper finest-numbered grit for the sandpaper to finish the preparation of his fingertips of one hand and the longer, shaped nails on the other.

His energy and dedication seemed boundless. After his audition, when he was actually offered a place in the program, his elation was just as boundless.

For each of his four years at Alma College, Tommy had to play for the juries to keep his scholarship. He always succeeded in winning his place in the program. Though he had had several other scholarships offered to

The Speech of Angels

him—Merit, Presidential, Musical Performance—it was always Alma College's opportunity for the study of the classical guitar that won Tommy's commitment.

At home, Tommy usually had a guitar strapped on, as if it were and item of clothing—his at-home uniform. The ones not being worn were all over the house, usually hogging the chairs. Human guests often had to wait for guitars to be moved to make seating room.

Of the four chairs in the living room, three might have guitars in them—sitting very upright on their plump, round bottoms, craning their long, skinny necks, as if trying to catch Tommy's attention. Vicki can still picture that series of movements Tommy had to perform to separate from a guitar.

If he heard, "Tommy, come and eat", he would stick the pick (if he were using one for this practice) in his mouth, bring the strap over his head, remove the pick from his mouth and slide it between the strings and the frets, then seat the guitar, as if it were a friend who would have to wait for him to finish eating before they could resume their play.

Vicki must have watched that routine hundreds of

The Speech of Angels

times—maybe a thousand—and each time she thought: *One of these days, he's going to swallow that pick.* If he ever did choke on it, he never admitted it to Vicki.

Even after the first year of college, when Tommy moved out of the family home, the guitars remained there. It was convenient, while he attended Alma College, for Tommy to drive north to the house to practice. Or, if he wanted to head south to Ann Arbor to visit Tony at the University of Michigan, he would take a couple of guitars with him.

He often took guitars to other places to play, but they **lived** at home, where they would be safe from harm. They were too important to his studies to risk their safety in the outside world. When Gary and Vicki moved to the house on Fancher Street, the guitars moved with them.

Tommy's dedication, hard work, and talent resulted in the successful completion of his studies. He would have walked to receive his diploma on April 23, 1994--two days after he was killed. The College awarded him his diploma posthumously, calling his name at the ceremony in recognition of his achievement. They sent a

The Speech of Angels

video tape to Gary and Vicki, but, though the gesture was well meant, neither one of them has ever been able to watch it.

Vicki said they couldn't bear the idea of hearing his name announced,and then seeing an empty platform and hearing only silence--knowing Tommy would never respond.

The Speech of Angels
Chapter Ten

After he had completed his studies at Alma College, Tommy was probably somewhat intimidated by his future. His heartfelt ambition certainly would have been to bring his education and talent to fruition by performing Classical Guitar for appreciative audiences, but, in practicality, he needed to find summer employment to earn money.

On that afternoon of April 21st, 1994, he had been working on filling out an application for a job at LaBelle Management, a local company which managed several restaurants in the area. He filled in his first name as "Tom", which, most likely, was what most of his friends called him and the name he would prefer at any place of employment, though his family still called him "Tommy". He entered the telephone number at his apartment on Broadway, but also wrote his parents' number, as an alternate. He was often at their house, and, if he weren't there or at home, his mother or dad would be certain to get a message to him so he wouldn't miss a job opportunity. He checked "Yes" that he was between the

The Speech of Angels

ages of 18 and 70, "Yes" that he had his own auto and supplied his driver's license number. He checked boxes that assured he could work days, nights, and week-ends and that he desired a position as bartender or set-up. He gave his educational information: Graduate of Mount Pleasant High School, completing a "General" curriculum, and had earned a degree with a major in music at Alma College.

Tommy was no doubt full of ambition and hope that he would, in time, have a satisfying career, but was realistically applying for work where his education and talent may be meaningless, but the pay would help with expenses when he started graduate school in the fall. Eventually, he would find an opportunity which would bring him closer to fulfilling his dream.

His application was never turned in. Perhaps, in the midst of working on it, he remembered that he had planned to attend Earth Day activities at Central Michigan University that afternoon. He set the form aside, probably planning to complete it the next day, and headed to the campus.

The Speech of Angels

Earth Day at CMU is a well-attended event--by students and alumni, as well as local residents. The popularity of the event, coupled with the warmer-than-usual weather, had attracted a very large crowd to the campus. Despite the throng, Tommy caught sight of his former girlfriend on the campus mall that day.

They had dated for a year, but, about a month earlier, she had told him that she couldn't continue to see him unless he sought help for the depression which sometimes gripped him and had caused difficulties with their relationship.

After leaving the campus that evening, Tommy stopped at a local bar with friends, and, perhaps emboldened by the drinks he had consumed, he telephoned to ask her about a reconciliation.

Since he had recently sought treatment at the Department of Neuropsychiatry at the University of Michigan, and had been taking the antidepressant the doctor had prescribed, he asked if she would consent to see him again. She was reluctant, however, and declined .

The Speech of Angels

Tommy called her back several times, but she would not speak with him further. He apparently decided he shouldn't persist any further that night. He also must have realized that he should not drive after the drinks he had consumed. Leaving his car on Main Street across from the bar, Tommy began walking to his parents' house, only a few blocks away.

They were usually home in the evening, and he had been spending much time there lately, often staying overnight, so there was no need to call to tell them he was on his way.

They'd realize that he'd been drinking, and Dad would want to know where he had left the car. His mom would probably insist, in her combination scolding/caring tone, that he sit at the kitchen table and have something to eat. (Vicki had indeed prepared something extra for his dinner, in case he came by.)

Then, they would sit with him, and listen to him, and, even though they'd understand his disappointment and express sympathy for him, they would probably advise him to be patient and give both his treatment and his former girlfriend more time.

The Speech of Angels

But, his parents weren't at home when he arrived. They had received a call from his girlfriend's mother, who had expressed concern for his emotional state because of his phone calls to her daughter.

Gary and Vicki became alarmed and went immediately to her apartment, thinking Tommy may be heading over there. They could intercept him and bring him home, where he could recover his emotional stability. However, when they found he was not at her place, Gary and Vicki had split up and each went in search of their son.

Shortly after nine o'clock, Gary returned to the house. He entered the breezeway, but the door into the kitchen, which they routinely left open, was now locked. Looking through the window of the kitchen door, he saw blood on the floor. He ran across the alley to a neighbor's house and asked him to call 911 for an ambulance—that he feared Tommy may be trying to harm himself. An ambulance was dispatched to the Sova residence at 9:27 P.M., arriving at 9:32---accompanied by several police officers.

The Speech of Angels

Tommy Sova, a talented, dedicated, loving young man, died little more than an hour from this point. Vicki, shortly after returning to a scene of chaos and flashing lights around her house, heard the shots from where she stood on the lawn.

She began screaming hysterically and collapsed. The ambulance, summoned to the scene by a distraught father to rescue his injured son, instead transported Vicki to the hospital, while Tommy, already beyond any need of medical help, lay motionless and silent in their home.

The Speech of Angels
Chapter Eleven

It is difficult to comprehend the depth of shock and grief a family would endure after the death of their son in any manner, but these circumstances—deadly violence against a suicidal young man, already staggered by too much alcohol, loss of blood, and being sprayed with Mace, not only compounded the family's grief, but put them in the midst of a community-wide controversy.

An explosion of newspaper stories, columns, letters to the editor, telephone calls, and intrusive publicity added a whirlwind of dismay, horror, and confusion to a family in deep shock and mourning.

A quiet aura of sympathy and empathy from family members and close friends was difficult to achieve when the manner of their son's death had been so shocking and continued to be a matter of public concern and comment for months.

We will never know why Tommy became self-destructive that night. We do know he made a bad decision when he drank a quantity of alcohol, but, even so, he didn't get behind the wheel and place fellow

The Speech of Angels

drivers at risk. Even though the warm spring day had begun a typical Michigan hyperbolic temperature swing and was dropping down to twenty degrees, he had decided to walk home.

He was going to the place, home, and the people, his parents, where he would find help and comfort. Despite his earlier emotional reaction when speaking to his former girlfriend, he had since made logical and responsible decisions to refrain from driving and to return home to seek his parents' help.

After years of study, practice, and incredible dedication and rational determination, he had achieved the skills and knowledge he needed to perform the music which satisfied his creativity and inspired his soul.

If he were lucky, it may even earn him a living. He should have been filled with a sense of optimism and accomplishment. But, instead, Tommy was fighting thoughts of despair and suicide, which seemed to be overwhelming him.

He had come home to the love and hope he had always found there, and which may have comforted him enough to calm his terrors and overcome this suicidal

The Speech of Angels

compulsion. None of the cuts he had inflicted upon himself were serious wounds, though he had lost a quantity of blood.

Instead, as his Certificate of Death testifies: Thomas John Sova died, at 10:45 PM, as a result of "homicide"...."within minutes"...after "a gunshot wound of chest," in which a Black Talon Type bullet had "torn a hole through his heart."

A brutally brief, official description of the end of a young man's life and the beginning of years of grief for those who loved him.

The Speech of Angels

The Speech of Angels
Chapter Twelve

Gary and Vicki still live in the house where Tommy was killed. People often seemed surprised that they would have remained there, and (after a decent length of time, one hopes) real estate agents had contacted them to inquire if they were interested in selling their house.

They remain in their home for the many happy memories it holds—not for the few minutes of horror that were imposed upon it. Tommy, after many years of bringing wonderful music and pride to their home, did not intentionally bring such tragedy into their home and lives.

For a while after Tommy's death, Vicki stayed up at their cottage. It was peaceful there, but, even as she said her daily rosary in the quiet privacy, she longed to be back home. She didn't think of their home only as the place Tommy had died, but where he had lived, and the family who had nurtured and loved Tommy should continue to live there. "I can't envision that anyone else would be in this house where my Tommy died," she explained.

The Speech of Angels

After Vicki returned home and had decided to go back to teaching, she found it very difficult to resume her previous life. "It was so hard for me to go to school." She needed to prepare herself emotionally each morning. She always brought her coffee to the little "chapel" room upstairs, where she would sit quietly, gathering enough inner strength to face the day.

One morning, she distinctly heard someone say: "They're still here." She didn't think she had dozed off, and the voice seemed so clear—it didn't seem like part of a dream. It had felt so real; she thought about it a lot, but wasn't sure what it was supposed to mean.

Another time, as she sat in the chapel, she saw something, someone, flit by in the hall at the foot of the stairs. A sudden impression came to her mind: There were angels in the house—the ones who had come for Tommy. Though Vicki had never read or studied anything about angels coming for people's spirits at death, this sudden, unbidden impression seemed very strong. Would they remain at or revisit the site of death? Vicki had thought Tommy died in the kitchen, but she later learned that he had staggered to the hall and died in the stairwell.

The Speech of Angels

After having had these strong feelings about the angels, she became more adamant about the house and not wanting to part with it.

Gary and Vicki subsequently received a letter from a man who had once lived in the house. He was asking their permission to visit what had once been his home. He had come there to live after his father was killed on New Year's Eve, 1944 and was hoping they would allow him to visit the home he had grown to love and which held many pleasant memories.

Vicki invited him to the house, and he was gratified to see how well the home of his childhood memories had fared. Gary had been working on the house and had burnished its beauty without changing its 1930's character. His years of helping to care for the floors and furniture and fixtures of the old Main Tavern had brought his skills to good use.

During their conversation, Gary and Vicki learned that their guest's grandfather had died in their kitchen, in the early 1950's, after suffering a sudden fatal heart attack. When Vicki heard that the date this had happened was April 20th, she told her guest that Tommy had died in the

The Speech of Angels

house on April 21st. Upon comparing their birthdays, they found that the grandfather had been born on November 14th, while Tommy's birthday was November 15th. They had each lived exactly five months and six days into that final year of their lives. They also have in common that their deaths were sudden and premature.

The grandfather would have ordinarily lived another decade or two, while Tommy had most of his life before him, and they each are sadly missed and deeply mourned, despite the years that have passed.

Thomas John Sova, even now, should yet have had many years of music and laughter and accomplishment to share with his family. His mother and father will never have that deadly night fade from their memories. His brother will always feel the gap in his life that Tommy would have filled with a brother's love and companionship.

His many family members and friends will miss him and will never forget the kind, helpful, talented, somewhat shy and quiet (except with his guitars) young man he was.

The Speech of Angels

Mental wounds not healing
Who and what's to blame?
I'm going off the rails
On a Crazy train...

Ozzie Osbourne's
Crazy Train

Author's Comment:

This is the story of Tom Sova's life, and, as such, I have not included the details of the night he died. My hope is that his parents, Vicki and Gary, his brother, Tony, and other family members and friends who loved him would be able to read his story of dedication, commitment, and accomplishment without the intrusion of another recounting of that night's violence.

For more information visit his family's website:

www.thomasjohnsova.com

The Speech of Angels

Epilogue

After that night of April 21st, 1994, *The Morning Sun*, Mount Pleasant's daily paper, published many news stories, opinion pieces, letters to the editor, and guest columns about what had happened at the Sova home that night. While most people understood the tragedy of a young man losing his life, it had become a controversial topic when the issue of the actions of the police is raised.

Each year, Gary and Vickie publish a memorial photo of Tommy and a brief commentary about him on the anniversary of his birth, November 15th and on April 21st, the date of his death. These remembrances often inspire comment from readers, whose thoughts range from sympathy and outrage, to "time to get over it" advice.

On April 25th, 2010, Rick Mills, Executive Editor of *The Morning Sun*, published an opinion piece, as follows:

A Mother Remembers her Son:

Tom Sova was a pretty good kid—a shy boy and an avid reader with exceptional musical talent. Most likely, you've never heard that before.

The Speech of Angels

Gary and Vicki Sova loved their son Tom like any parent loves any child. They will miss him every single day of their lives.

For those of us who report or consume the news, big stories fade into our collective memories. Perhaps that is Vicki Sova's greatest fear—that all these years later, her son is remembered only as the drunk young man shot by police on the back porch of his family home.

A community's memory may fade, but a mother's memory—especially of the worst day of her life—does not.

"Sixteen years later, it is all as painful as it was then," Vicki wrote to me. "There is no recovery for this family."

On that fateful night, the Sovas returned home to find blood on their porch and a locked house. They called for an ambulance, and minutes later their son was dead in a series of events perhaps as horrific as any this town has ever seen.

Even all these years later, merely writing about that night in April, 1994 is certain to reopen wounds and

The Speech of Angels

reinvigorate the side-taking. That is not my intention, and that should not be the community's intention.

But to ponder a mother's pain is certainly worth the time invested.

"All I want is for Tom's image to be somewhat restored to what it was all his life—except for the last ten minutes," Vicki wrote. "He really was as an extremely bright and talented boy."

Here are some memories shared by a mother for whom the grief never will never end:

"He was shy and had beautiful eyes. In high school mock elections, he was voted the shyest boy and the boy with the most beautiful eyes. He was very popular with all the students—not just his group. He was on the King's Court as a senior. He was kind and had an amazing sense of humor.

"Tom was granted a full ride scholarship to Alma College for Classical guitar.

"Tom's favorite guitar players were Allen Holdsworth, Al Demiloa, Jeff Beck, Robin Ford, and Tommy Bolin. I could watch Tom listening to Allen Holdsworth and I could see it in his face that something

The Speech of Angels

was amazing. Tom would say, 'Mom, he just did something no one should be able to do.'

"Good guitar players know these musicians. Tom's interest was fusion," his mother wrote.

"We all have dreams for our children. For the Sovas, one of those dreams occurred when Tom graduated from college—posthumously, two days after he died.

Vicki knows there's nothing she can do about those dreams anymore. Instead she has just one request: That a community reconsider her son's memory. I can do that. Maybe you can, too."

Posted to the newspaper's website in response to the above article: "The following are comments from the readers. In no way do they represent the view of *themorningsun.com:*"

On April 25th:cm1234 wrote: "I have never forgotten. Although I did not have the opportunity to know him in high school, I did get that chance after graduation. Tom was a very kind, genuine, and funny individual."

The Speech of Angels

mphs1989 wrote: "Mrs. Sova, I would like you to know that I think about Tommy every day. I was lucky enough to know him from 7th grade on. I remember him playing guitar in our talent show and he awed the crowd and myself. He never had a bad word to say about anyone, and always had a smile on his face."

Irish wrote: "I never knew Tommy personally, but I watched him grow up, just by seeing him around town over the years. Strikingly handsome, with those beautiful eyes. The majority of the city mourned him...many of us still do. Our city lost its innocence that night. My continued sympathy to Tom's parents and family."

On April 26th:

Morningsunid1972 wrote: "Dear Mrs. Sova, The community has not forgotten your beautiful son. We cannot imagine your pain..."

jfortinofish wrote: "I read the article about my beautiful nephew Tommy and my sister Vicki! We are all grateful for it. No one has ever suffered more than my sister at any loss...."

vcfortin wrote: "Tommy was my cousin and there is not another person that I have ever known that I miss as much as him. He was the most humble, fun

The Speech of Angels

and beautiful person that I have ever known.... Despite having incredible talent, he was not interested in showing off...he was only interested in playing the guitar because he loved it. I think...(he) was humble and that is a rare trait. ....He was one of the best influences that I had in my life and I loved and respected him more than anyone. I think since this event happened I have only been home to Mt. Peasant a handful of times and I know in my heart it is because I really don't want to be there because he is not there anymore. Mount Pleasant really lost one of its best that horrible night and one thing I pray for almost daily is that I will get a chance to see him again in Heaven. He was the best and I will never forget him or all of the good times we had."

On April 27th:mcg wrote: " Dear Mrs. Sova and all of Tommy's relatives, This town has not forgotten what happened that night and never will. I didn't know Tommy very well but I remember him coming in to help out in your classroom. He was a very nice guy! God bless all of you."

Dynamo of Volition Wrote: "Such a terrible tragedy to happen to such a wonderful family. His older

The Speech of Angels

brother used to babysit me (and so did Tom on occasion) when I was little.

I used to have the biggest crush on those boys! ...I'll never forget when I heard the news in my 1st hr. history class in junior high. ...I just hope that one day, the family is finally able to find some peace. If anyone deserves it, it is them. RIP Tommy."

jmeier wrote: "Vickie, I think of Tom often. He was one of my closest friends since the 7th grade. We shared a lot of great times together. I still have the guitar I played with him when we got together at your house. (Although he was so good I finally gave up and just watched and listened!) Tom really was a sweet and gentle soul. I'm glad to see the article bring this forward. Hope to see you someday."

gtravis wrote: "Tommy was my older cousin. When he was murdered I was eight years old.

Because I was so young, I don't remember him as well as I wish I could. But I do remember his calm, handsome presence and thinking that he was so cool with his long dark hair and his acid wash jeans (it was the early 90's, what can I say?) And I also remember, very clearly, how quickly our family was absolutely

The Speech of Angels

devastated. We lost so much in such a short amount of time.

I wish I could have gotten the chance to grow up around you, Tommy. I would have loved to hear you play guitar and we all wish we could have watched you take your talent to the top. Love, Gina"

<u>On April 28th</u>: <u>Phoebe wrote</u>: "Thank you Rick Mills for the remembrance of Tommy Sova the way we knew him. We all miss him very much and will never know why he was killed. He'd committed no crime."

The Speech of Angels

Segovia, My Book of the Guitar

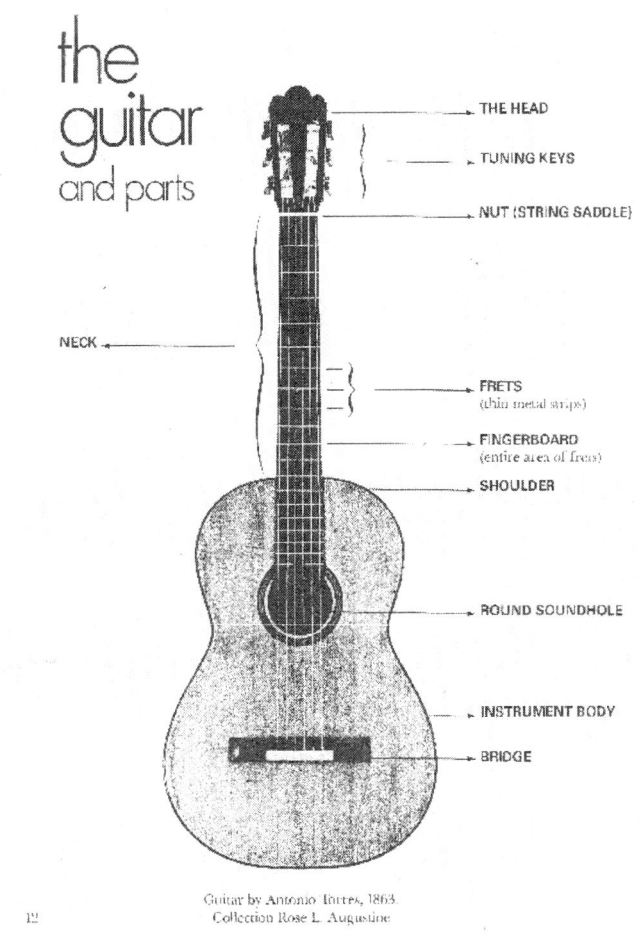

Illustration from Tommy's first study book.

The Speech of Angels

Thomas John Sova

November 15, 1970 – April 21, 1994

The Speech of Angels

The Speech of Angels

Acknowledgements:

The information for the histories of Gary's and Vicki's families is from their own prodigious memories. That background information and the details of their own and their son's lives, were given in the form of oral history to the author.

<u>Other Sources and References</u>:

This Place Mount Pleasant, © 1989, **by John Cumming.**

Legacies of Isabella's Early Indian Reservation, 1855-1872, Draft 2/2000, **by Hudson Keenan.**

Storms and Other Extreme Weather Events in Central Michigan © 1999, **by Hudson Keenan.**

Segovia, My Book of the Guitar, by **Andres Segovia and George Mendoza,** Ariel Publications, England

<u>Newspapers:</u> (Dates as Noted in Text)

The Mount Pleasant Times, Mount Pleasant , MI
The Enterprise, Mount Pleasant, MI
The Morning Sun, Mt. Pleasant and Alma, MI

And,

Thank You:

Amy, Cheryl, and Don (my writer's group) for their advice and encouragement.

The Speech of Angels

The Speech of Angels

Perplexed Music

Experience, like a pale musician, holds
A dulcimer of patience in his hand,
Whence harmonies, we cannot understand,
Of God; will in his worlds, the strain unfolds
In sad-perplexed minors: deathly colds
Fall on us while we hear, and countermand
Our sanguine heart back from the fancyland
With nightingales in visionary wolds.
We murmur ' Where is any certain tune
Or measured music in such notes as these ?
But angels, leaning from the golden seat,
Are not so minded their fine ear hath won
The issue of completed cadences,
And, smiling down the stars, they whisper--
SWEET.

                        Elizabeth Barrett Browning

Made in the USA
Charleston, SC
06 February 2014